# FASHION
## A CRASH COURSE

# FASHION
## A CRASH
## COURSE

ANDREW TUCKER
TAMSIN KINGSWELL

SIMON & SCHUSTER
A VIACOM COMPANY

First published in Great Britain by
Simon & Schuster UK Ltd, 2000
A Viacom Company

1 3 5 7 9 10 8 6 4 2

SIMON & SCHUSTER UK LTD
Africa House
64-78 Kingsway
London WC2B 6AH

SIMON & SCHUSTER AUSTRALIA
Sydney

A CIP catalogue record for this book is
available from the British Library

ISBN 0-684-86663-3

*This book was conceived, designed
and produced by*
THE IVY PRESS LIMITED
The Old Candlemakers, West Street
Lewes, East Sussex, BN7 2NZ

*Art Director:* PETER BRIDGEWATER
*Editorial Director:* DENNY HEMMING
*Designer:* JANE LANAWAY
*Editor:* GRAPEVINE PUBLISHING SERVICES
*DTP Designers:* CHRIS LANAWAY, TRUDI VALTER
*Picture Research:* VANESSA FLETCHER
*Illustrations:* MADELEINE HARDIE

Printed and bound in China

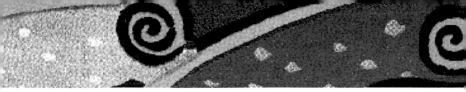

# Contents

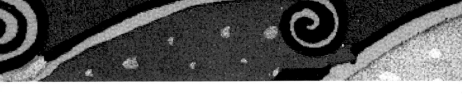

# Introduction

*While no one could accuse fashion of being as serious as, say, the quest for world peace or brain surgery, whether we like it or not, the clothes that we wear are an enormously powerful statement that can reveal more about us than anything we may say or do. Fashion is essentially a form of tribalism and a way of giving clear messages about who we are, so it is not surprising that people can have an abiding fascination with something as apparently superficial as a hat or a handbag – even if it's not their own.*

*The 20th century has also proved to be the most fashion-conscious century so far, with the appreciation of clothes reaching a far greater audience through the development of mass-market production techniques and improved communications. Clothing has become a kind of visual currency that people understand and want to buy into.*

**How this course works**

Each double-page spread is devoted to a type of clothing, style movement, designer or group of designers with something in common, and the story proceeds more or less chronologically. On each spread there are some regular features. It won't take you long to figure them out but check the boxes on pages 8–11 for more information.

Shock! Horror! New Look frocks used up to 80 yards of fabric in the era of postwar rationing.

Witness the enormous growth in aspirational brands in the 1980s and the near deification of models that began in the 1960s. Fashion designers like Chanel, Donna Karan and Calvin Klein have also been elevated to household names, as was illustrated by the acres of news coverage when Italian designer Versace was shot and killed outside his palatial Miami mansion.

Weighing just six and a half stone, Twiggy became the first supermodel in the 1960s.

Fashion for all may not be the most important development in the 20th century, but in commercial terms it has a lot of clout (and it is arguable that Calvin Klein underwear is of more interest to the youth of today than man landing on the Moon). What we have tried to do in this book is to look at fashion in context, as anthropology, frivolity and as art.

Rap singer Marky Mark has a close relationship with his Calvins.

**FASHION ESSENTIALS**

The must-have items that no fashion victim should be without, plus tips on recreating the designer look. Spot a Chanel jacket at 50 paces and make sure you're wearing the right trainers.

*Fashion has permeated virtually every major event this century, from war to Woodstock. In a world that increasingly deals with the visual metaphor, how people look is important and fashion provides the tools. It would be impossible to think of the 1960s without the mini skirt or Kennedy's assassination without Jackie Kennedy's blood-stained Chanel suit, or even the conflicts in Vietnam without that camouflaged look.*

*What fashion manages to do with unerring accuracy is reveal the mood of the time, providing a perfect record of the emotional state of the world. It cannot be seen as an accident that boyish figures and taped-down*

Audrey Hepburn takes it easy in a slinky little Givenchy number.

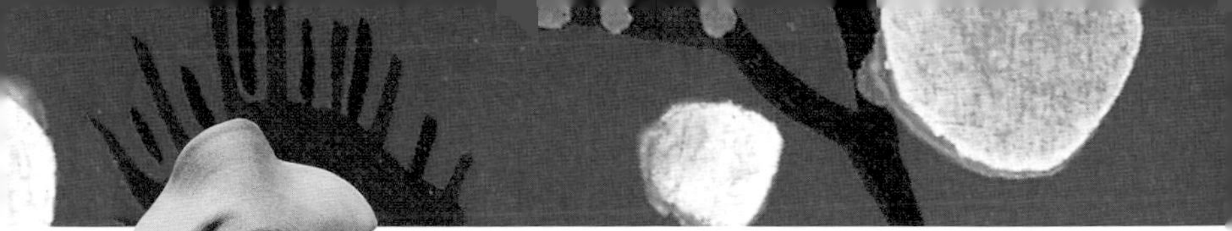

breasts in the 1920s followed the
cataclysmic culling of European men
in the First World War;
that body hair and
sloganed T-shirts
were used as a
political statement by
the blossoming feminist
movement in the 1970s; or
that yuppies liked shoulder
pads and big hair.
This book is
an admittedly partisan attempt to
reveal how fashion and the mood of the
time fit hand in delicately embroidered
kid skin glove and that to ignore the
influence of what we wear is to ignore a
vital element of 20th-century culture.

*Tamsin Kingswell*

TAMSIN KINGSWELL

Shiver me timbers!
Westwood's New
Romantic pirate look.

**Timeline**
More of a contextual
chronology than a
timeline, because
designers and
movements are
constantly overlapping.
A selected list of major
events happening at
the time the styles were
popular, to illuminate
the world clothes were
displayed in.

The Material Girl forgets
to put a dress on top of
her underwear again.

**1851** At the Great Exhibition in London, British surgeon Nathaniel Ward displays a fern that has lived for twenty years in an airtight glass jar and starts a craze for terrariums.

**1862** Victor Hugo publishes his 10-volume work *Les Misérables* from his home on Guernsey, after being banished from France by Napoleon III.

**1873** Mary Ann Cotton is hanged for murder in Durham. She killed up to twenty people, including her husband and children, by poisoning them with arsenic.

1850s~1880s

# Know Your Worth

## Fashion's first couturier

Bright young things get into a flap over Worth's 1921 collection.

*It's hard to believe that when he set off to Paris at the tender age of twenty, with a fiver in his pocket, Lincolnshire lad Charles WORTH (1825–95) was about to change the face of fashion. But if this reads like the synopsis for a Barbara Taylor Bradford blockbuster, that's no apology for the birth of fashion's first designer, a man who set taste levels and trends in a way that the court dressmakers and seamstresses of the nobility could only aspire to in the mid 19th century.*

Although there is a certain irony in the fact that the founding father of fashion was an Englishman in the most fiercely Gallic of cities, Worth gravitated there to join the prestigious firm of Gagelin, Paris's most famous silk merchant. During his eleven years with the company, he transformed the all-male bastion into a fashion hot spot, by staging the industry's first fashion show with models wearing simple dresses designed to better display the company's silks. These simple creations soon became top of the wanted list for history's first fashion victims. As a result, Worth was able to establish the first designer atelier, which, despite the reservations of his employers, soon became a kind of 19th-century version of a hip boutique.

Worth became increasingly influential and in 1858 he decided to go it alone, initially opening with a partner from the same company, like a Victorian version of Dolce & Gabbana. Success followed swiftly, ultimately including the accolade of royal patronage from Empress Eugenie, the Jackie Kennedy of her day and a woman who could alter the fortunes of the fabric industry with a single choice of material.

**Gross Worth**

Worth became so successful that by 1870 he was employing over 1,200 seamstresses, turning out hundreds of dresses a week and making a clear profit of £40,000 a year. And even if the fabrics for his most prominent clients' gowns were subsidized from the designer's own pocket, this subtle form of advertising brought him more of the chic and wealthy clientèle he needed. Not bad going for a guy who slept under the counter in his first job.

**1877** Cornelius Vanderbilt leaves a record $100 million in his will.

**1880** Cologne Cathedral, the largest in Europe, is completed after 634 years of work.

**1889** A Georgia clothing store takes out an advert in the local paper. It will run every day until August 1987, a total of 35,291 adverts.

Mind you don't trip! Not the most practical dress for an illicit assignation in the park.

Other spectacular successes included the fabled peacock dress created for the Princess de Sagan to wear to the Animal Ball of 1864, that was an orgy of exotic feathers including a life-like head-dress, and the humbler renditions of national costumes that had started the craze back at Gagelin's.

Although his expensive and ostentatious gowns were very much in demand from the *nouveau riche* of the 1860s, Worth was not just a showman. He radicalized the female silhouette, dropping waists and hemlines, doing away with shawls and bonnets, and introducing two of the defining elements in late-19th-century womenswear – the puff skirt and the bustle. Despite continuing as a family-run company until a rival take-over bid in 1954, Worth is now best remembered as the first designer to present summer and winter collections, the first to use live models and the first to sell his designs as paper patterns for the export market (all cheques and postal orders payable to...). And if his designs look more like costume history than high fashion, his ideas – such as trimming 10 inches off the Empress's skirt length – were as radical as someone putting the present queen in hot pants, or Pamela Anderson in a baggy T-shirt.

### FASHION ESSENTIALS

It may look like a wedding cake to us bods but the gown that turned Worth into a 19th-century version of John Galliano was an intricate confection of tulle, daisies, pink hearts, bunches of wild grass and silver spangles. The silver tulle in the skirt cost more than 300 francs. The Austrian ambasssador's wife wore it to a state ball at the Tuileries, where it was noticed by the Empress Eugenie, who summoned Worth to the palace. The upshot – the most fashionable woman in Europe was no longer dressed by a humble dressmaker, but by a designer with a signature and a new profession was born.

The Victorian *nouveau riche* bustle along to the couture salons.

**1850** Only half of the children born in the US live to the age of five.

**1889** Louis Glass takes Edison's phonograph a step further by adding a coin-slot so that you 'pay to play'.

**1895** Devon residents find mysterious footprints in the snow one morning; they are 8 inches long, 2 inches across and were made by a biped. Locals think they are the devil's footprints.

## 1850~1914

# Trussed Busts and Bustles
## Victorian undergarments

What the butler saw – layers of unnecessary garments.

*It is astonishing that the sheer weight of Victorian ladies' underwear didn't bring them to their knees, and it also explains the need for smelling salts. Women in the 1850s were invariably burdened with long drawers, a flannel petticoat, an under petticoat, a petticoat wadded to the knees and stiffened by whalebone, a white starched petticoat, two muslin petticoats and finally the dress.*

**The Gibson Girl**
A character invented by illustrator Charles Dana Gibson in 1890, the Gibson Girl epitomized the tall Junoesque ideal woman, often seen engaging in healthy pursuits like cycling with brisk efficiency. Manufacturers of all sorts used her image in their advertising and, in 1907, The Ziegfeld Follies performed a revue entitled *The Gibson Bathing Girl*.

The S-bend in all its glory, causing unimaginable damage to women's backs.

Enter the crinoline, a sort of cage structure of light metal or whalebone that despite its bad press must have seemed like a breath of fresh air. Credited to Charles Worth *(see pages 12–13)*, the crinoline's origins remain obscure but by 1860 a Victorian woman wouldn't have been seen dead without one. As if crinolines weren't ridiculous enough, bodices reached new heights of impracticality as tight lacing became mandatory (you too could have an 18-inch waist if you didn't mind fainting at inconvenient moments).

Corsets followed and the bust was big news with everything pushed up and out (except for vital internal organs, which were squashed in). There was even interest in the first breast implants – artificial strap-on things made from

**1899** In the US, women's clothing costs $4 for a skirt, 35 cents for a blouse, 40 cents for a corset, $5 for a silk petticoat, 59 cents for a beaded purse.

**1901** Anarchist Leon Czolgosz shoots President William McKinley at the Buffalo Pan-American Exposition; the assassin dies in the electric chair later in the year.

**1905** Anna Pavlova dances the Dying Swan in St Petersburg.

pink rubber (less intrusive than today's silicone option). By the early 1870s the bustle, a kind of bizarre steel frame tied on at the waist, helped give the impression of an enormous bottom. It was perhaps not surprising that some women rejected all this discomfort and Pre-Raphaelite painters came to the rescue,

## FASHION ESSENTIALS

Drawers originally consisted of two separate sections, one for each leg, joined at the waist with a band. Several pairs of Queen Victoria's drawers have been sold at auction and were reported to resemble 'two great linen slings gaping at the front and held together by a drawstring'. Lucky old Albert – most men would pay good money to see that.

Brassieres were introduced in 1912 but not in the current form, being more of a bust bodice contraption. Later developments in America by Mary Phelps Jacob were softer and more bra-shaped, gathered between the breasts to give delineation. As skirts became slimmer, petticoats were adapted, becoming a fine tube with little bulk, and open knickers continued to live and breathe until the First World War when they were sewn up for good (or until Ann Summers started giving parties).

introducing the aesthetic movement as well as lots of pictures of women with long, flowing hair clutching flowers to their breasts.

Corsets were abandoned, sanitary woollen knickers embraced and bodices with soft bust sections were adopted with sighs of relief. In the 1880s, Dr Jaeger introduced comfy wool next to the skin, including dangerously asexual stockinet drawers and combinations. However you can't keep a woman from reaching for artifice for long and the Edwardian craze for S-bend corsets reached new heights of control and enabled them to fit into the Gibson Girl (see box) ideal of the day.

Letting it all hang loose in Rossetti's *The Daydream* (1880).

## STYLE ICON ★

*Born in Spain, **Empress Eugenie** (1826–1920) became a fashion leader upon her marriage to Napoleon III in 1853. She was obsessively copied by her court and every frill was noted and reproduced. Eugenie was a fan of crinolines and wore possibly the first ever seen in England when she visited Queen Victoria in 1855. Aided by the designer Charles Worth, her crinolines reached epic proportions before she dumped them in favour of a flat-fronted dress unsupported by a crinoline, creating a watershed after which everyone who was anyone consigned their crinolines to the fashion graveyard.*

**1892** In his book *How to Write a Popular Song*, composer, lyricist and publisher Charles Harris warns, 'Styles in songs change as quickly as ladies' millinery'.

**1933** Diego Rivera creates the mural *Man at the Crossroads* for New York's Radio City Music Hall.

**1981** A new shopping centre in Alberta, Canada, has over 800 shops, including 11 major department stores, making it the world's largest.

1900s~1990s

# Serious Shopping
## The department store

*Shopping as a form of recreation is, in my opinion, one of the greatest 20th-century inventions and it was first exploited by those great Edwardian temples to commerce – the palatial department stores.*

Shop till you drop.

## Chic to Cheek

In the early days, department stores' popularity was based on the speed at which they could import the latest styles from Paris. Edwin Goodman made frequent buying trips, and Debenham and Freebody successfully advertised original French gowns in 1928. In-store designers began copying French styles to provide a cheaper alternative (a practice that, to their dismay, was later adapted by street stallholders yelling 'Chanel Number 5, only two quid a bottle'). However by the Second World War the dominance of Parisian couture was broken in the US as designers like Clare McCardell *(see page 64)* advocated a more American style. Today department store buyers source from all over the world.

Bringing accessible fashion to the masses for the first time, many of the best-known department stores evolved in Britain from traditional haberdashers' or in the US from general hardware companies. Huge businesses were established in the early 20th century by wily entrepreneurs who saw that more and more people were becoming fashion-conscious, and that some women even had their own wage packets to pay for their new frocks.

So much choice and so little time: a shopper ponders outside Bloomingdale's, New York.

Tailor Herman Bergdorf joined forces with Edwin Goodman at the turn of the century; their emporium on New York's Fifth Avenue continues to be a shopping Mecca today. Neiman Marcus was founded in 1907 by Herbert Marcus and his sister and brother-in-law Mr and Mrs Neiman, to bring fashion to newly oil-rich Texas. In Britain, Harrods had evolved from a grocers' in 1849 to being the first to introduce that department store essential, the moving staircase, in 1898, making it

Setting a precedent: Edwardian ladies rush to the opening of the Harrods sale.

had clearly differentiated themselves from the multiples by promoting themselves as designer name emporiums, using innovative marketing strategies (and must-have carrier bags) to create the exclusivity vital for their survival (and an excuse to bump their prices up).

easier for customers to stagger around with multiple carrier bags. At the height of its popularity, when Debenham and Freebody rebuilt their department store in 1908 it was described as a 'palace' and one of the finest shops in the world.

These were halcyon days for department stores, who shipped in ready-to-wear fashion from Paris at breakneck speed, introduced the modern concept of window dressing with gawky plastic mannequins and had huge workrooms to service their clients' demands. But by the Second World War, multiples like Marks & Spencer had begun to chip away at the dominance of the departments. By the 1980s, prestige stores like Saks, Harrods, Harvey Nichols and Bergdorf Goodman

## STYLE ICON
★

*Built in 1909, with a central position on London's Oxford Street, **Selfridges** is the ultimate department store and the dream child of American Gordon Selfridge. While most other stores evolved slowly over time, Selfridges was purpose-built from scratch, and its original 120 staff were hired months before its opening. The shop was launched with 104 pages of advertising in newspapers and magazines nationwide, encouraging customers to spend the day browsing and enjoying that shopping experience. The interior was a model of today's department stores, with carefully flattering lighting, piped 'muzak' and fresh flowers, not to mention dedicated staff squirting perfume at unwary passersby. It is a testament to Selfridge's farsightedness that the shop's basic design remained unchanged until a cosmetic makeover in 1997.*

Who needs religion when Selfridges provides the ultimate shopping heaven?

1890s~present

# Sofa Shopping
## Mail order delivers fast fashion

*The ingenious concept of mail-order fashion began in America around the 1890s. Due to the sheer size of the country, many potential customers had limited access to clothing shops and this led to a crop of enterprising companies hitting on the idea of producing catalogues or full-page newspaper adverts of the latest styles, that they could then dispatch all over the country. Even if they never looked quite as good as they had on the model, and the sleeves were always too short, happy fashion-starved shoppers lapped them up.*

Get your corsets by pony express! Early catalogue shopping.

Sears catalogue offered these delightful snow suits (all of them Aridex treated).

The service quickly grew sophisticated. Siegel Cooper Co announced that every woman in America should be able to obtain unprecedented style by no less than the 'famous house of Paquin in Paris', while by 1908 Sears was offering 'elegant lacy lingerie dresses' for as little as $6. Sears Roebuck soon became the largest mail-order company in America, and has continued to provide fashion to the furthest reaches of the US ever since.

In Britain as early as 1870, Debenham & Freebody offered a mail-order service for everything from made-to-measure to ready-to-wear, but British mail order soon became chiefly the domain of the older working-class women providing easy

**1932** *Family Circle* magazine is launched and distributed in American supermarkets with delicious recipes for all the family.

**1954** Only 154 Americans now earn more than $1 million a year; in 1929, it was 513.

**1987** A US newspaper advert for vodka plays 'Jingle Bells' when opened.

access to cheap, mass-produced clothes. In an attempt to alter this age balance in the 1960s, Freemans employed pop star Lulu (of 1969 Eurovision Song Contest infamy with her hit song 'Boom Bang-a-Bang') to promote a new teenage line.

By the 1980s, 13 per cent of the total sales of British women and children's clothing was purchased through catalogues, helped by a subtle shift in their perception with the nifty introduction of designer lines. Jasper Conran, Benny Ong, Joseph, Red or Dead, Vivienne Westwood and Betty Jackson have all featured in catalogues. There has also been a growth in specialist niche catalogues, including Racing Green and Boden. Department stores and shops like Marks & Spencer are jumping on the bandwagon, offering glossy, beautifully photographed lifestyle catalogues to tempt even more money out of their time-pressed customers.

Tiny Glaswegian singer Lulu uses her big voice to promote Freemans fashions.

### The goggle box

As more shopping channels appear on cable TV networks by the hour, the choice is becoming overwhelming but quality is not always top of the range and prices aren't necessarily competitive. QVC is now the UK's biggest seller of 14-carat gold, and they also provide clothing and home appliances. B-list celebs are muscling in on the act, so if you're lucky you might catch the likes of Ivana Trump singing the praises of a glitzy costume jewellery range. Perfect for couch potatoes who don't have a life.

### E-SHOPPING

The electronic shopping sector could well be the future for home shopping, whether through television shopping channels, CD-Rom or the Internet. Companies like La Redoute and Freemans are experimenting with e-shopping and lots of designers have their own web sites where you can buy new styles with a trusty credit card. While not all sites are transactional it seems it is only a matter of time before shopping will be as easy as logging on, and not just for purchasing nerdy, navy-blue anoraks.

### FASHION ESSENTIALS

Legendary British retailers Marks & Spencer, launched in 1894, didn't get into mail order until the 1980s. Their home catalogue now sells all manner of clothing, saving many a pair of sore feet from trudging round for that extra pair of slacks or the classic undies sets.

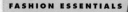

MARKS & SPENCER

M & S join the fray with their glossy lifestyle catalogue.

1800s~present

# Bespoken Like a Gent
## The kindest cut of all

*Savile Row has been a bastion of male sartorial elegance since the days of Beau BRUMMELL (1778–1840) and is at the heart of bespoke and custom tailoring in Britain as well as enjoying an international reputation. Edward VIII was a lifelong champion, and Oscar Wilde was undoubtedly thinking of Savile Row when he declared that a man's first duty was always to his tailor.*

Every sartorially inclined chap's dream: the haughty edifices of London's Savile Row.

**FASHION ESSENTIALS**

Gieves & Hawkes, over 200 years in the bespoke business, initially served military officers and gentlemen; they have branched out into ready-to-wear but still keep up a bespoke business. Huntsman was a breeches maker to the aristocracy and made distinctive slim-shaped jackets evolved from the hacking jacket. Kilgour French & Stanbury favoured smooth handle wool along with wool merino wool, alpaca and cashmere. Hardy Amies set up his business dressing members of the royal family from his classic atelier at number 14.

Savile Row is where the British tailored suit has been honed and perfected over 200 years. This is men's clothing as a craft, with the individual garment fitted and adjusted to enclose even the most corpulent figure to perfection. Savile Row style reached its heights in the 1930s, when they featured innovation hand in hand with tradition with the introduction of, among other items, the must-have multi-seasonal flannel suit. Post-war recovery was slow and laborious despite (or maybe because of) the patronage of politicians and presidents including Harold Macmillan and John F. Kennedy.

By the 1960s Savile Row had lost out to the hip appeal of Carnaby Street and had not adequately adjusted to the changing trends in men's clothing (Savile Row tailors couldn't quite bring themselves to address the tailoring issues of Y-shaped underwear and belted trousers). Even Tommy Nutter, tailor to stars such as Mick and Bianca Jagger and Twiggy, couldn't save them. (The Beatles may not have been renowned as aficionados of the pinstripe but they still recorded at the Apple Studios at Number 3 Savile Row.)

**1956** Julie Andrews and Rex Harrison star in the musical *My Fair Lady*, singing the songs 'I'm Getting Married in the Morning' and 'Why Can't the English Teach their Children How to Speak?'.

**1978** *The Times* and *The Sunday Times* suspend publication for eleven months in a dispute with the printers' unions.

**1984** When 58-stone Peter Yarnall of London dies, firemen have to break down the wall of his bedroom and winch his body out.

## GOSSIP

Cary Grant had his suits made by Kilgour, French & Stanbury, who obligingly padded his shoulders to make his head look smaller. Jack Buchanan happily crossed the Atlantic to get his suits from Scholte's in the 1920s. Not all Hollywood legends could get past the famous Savile Row snobbery, however. When Fred Astaire wanted suits made by the Prince of Wales's tailor Hawes & Curtis, he was flatly refused on the grounds that he worked in show business. In the end he had to go to Anderson & Sheppherd who, if not patronized by the prince, were at least still part of the Row.

Inside the hallowed portals of Gieves & Hawkes, where tradition is scrupulously observed.

Women get in on the act, but tailors turn in their graves to see suits worn without ties.

The bespoke suit enjoyed a renaissance in the 1980s with the conspicuous display of the yuppie, and continues today to be regarded as one of Britain's biggest style statements, despite production being absolutely tiny. The support of foreign clientele is vital to the continued success of the Row, as roughly three out of every four Savile Row suits are bought by visitors who can afford the price tag of around £1,000 upwards for a bespoke suit.

The spirit of Savile Row is kept alive by a new generation of British tailors, including *Ozwald* BOATENG (b. 1967), *Timothy* EVEREST (b. 1961), *Richard* JAMES (b. 1953) and *Mark* POWELL (b. 1960), who have popularized the Savile Row cut and the bespoke suit for an eager new generation of wearers.

**1900** A frozen mammoth is discovered standing upright in the Arctic permafrost in Siberia; its stomach contains undigested food and it has fresh buttercups in its mouth.

**1909** Selfridges department store opens in London's Oxford Street.

**1920** Croydon airport becomes the London airport for flights to and from the Continent.

1900~present
# The Mac and Welly Set
## Country casuals

Protection from the elements to major British export: 100 years in the life of Burberry.

*Although designers such as Westwood, McQueen and Galliano personify a new breed of Britishness (see pages 136-7), our heritage is not rooted in experimental design, but in sturdy waterproofs, hacking tweeds and jolly green wellington boots. Think of the British countryside and our perception is one of Barbour jackets, mackintoshes and gruff horsy folk with front teeth that have never heard the word 'orthodontist', tramping country lanes accompanied by a pair of bouncy Labradors.*

An average of 100,000 Burberry mackintoshes a year are sold worldwide, and the green waxed Barbour jacket has been around since 1870. All owe their origins to Scotsman *Charles MACKINTOSH* (1760–1843) who in 1830 developed a technique for mixing

The British ruling classes are inseparable from their horses (some of them even look like horses).

**1937** Britain introduces the 999 telephone code for calling the police, fire or ambulance services.

**1951** Premier Supermarkets opens the first British supermarket chain with a store in Earl's Court, London.

**1975** The term Sloane Ranger is coined to denote the young upper-classes who have homes in London and the country and wear expensive but casual clothes.

coal tar with rubber to form a waterproof solution, which was then used to coat traditionally permeable fabrics. The upshot? A rainproof garment that fast became popular despite its unwieldy shape and the extremely unpleasant smell of the first prototypes.

Inevitably the mack has become more sophisticated since the days of the open-topped carriage and the Sherlock Holmes novel. Today it is more than a coat rack essential for surviving inclement weather: it is a cult item with a versatility that transcends its classic connotations. From the classic Burberry and Aquascutum raincoats to the deluxe versions offered by Louis Vuitton, the mackintosh is equally as appropriate for old ladies feeding pigeons in the park as it is for pop stars and celebrities (and well-heeled flashers). Famous archetypes include the Sloane Ranger, for whom the Barbour jacket is a uniform of social acceptance, worn with a string of pearls, a cashmere twinset and a plummy accent, or the city trader in a charcoal suit and raincoat.

## STYLE ICON
★

*Movie Stars in Burberry:*
• *Audrey Hepburn and Humphrey Bogart* • *Gary Cooper and Joan Crawford in* Today We Live *(1933)* • *Jacques Tati in* Mon Oncle *(1958)* • *George Peppard in* Operation Crossbow *(1965)* • *Julie Andrews in* Torn Curtain *(1966)* • *George C. Scott in* Patton *(1970)* • *Robert Mitchum in* Farewell My Lovely *(1975)* • *Meryl Streep in* Kramer vs. Kramer *(1979)* • *Michael Douglas in* Wall Street *(1988)* • *Warren Beatty in* Dick Tracey *(1990)* • *In the film* The Pink Panther Strikes Again *(1976) Peter Sellers kept two Burberrys on set in case one was ruined during filming.*

In the 1990s, country clothing has been rejuvenated. Burberry employed ex-Montana and Jil Sander designer *Roberto MENICHETTI* (b. 1961) to revamp its countrified look and offer something to a more urban clientele. The result: a catwalk collection that owed little to the country squire and more to his 'it girl' daughter, heralding a new horizon for the country market. No doubt Range Rovers, head scarves and wellies will always play a role in the life of the rural aristocracy, but perhaps they'll be combined with a little fashion awareness too.

**1909** Frank Lloyd Wright completes the famous Robie House in Chicago, with room overhangs calculated to allow maximum light in winter and maximum shade in summer.

**1910** Father's Day is celebrated for the first time. It is the idea of Mrs John Bruce Dodd, whose father raised six children on his own after his wife died young.

**1911** The song 'Everybody's Doin' It' by Irving Berlin popularizes the Turkey Trot dance.

**1912** The first electric iron is produced by German company Rowenta.

1909~1914

# The Art of Dressing
## Ballet, illustration and antiquities

*Nikolai Cherepin's Narcisse wrestling with boa constrictors in floral chiffon.*

*The turn of the century was an exciting time to be in Paris. As the epicentre of art and performance, Paris ruled supreme (and didn't hesitate to tell the rest of the world so). Art was everywhere and fashion designers were becoming increasingly excited by the possibility of translating the latest artistic trends into pieces for their collections (easier than thinking up original ideas but I'm sure that wasn't the point).*

At the cutting edge of this fusion was the illustrator *Paul IRIBE* (1883–1935) who created a brochure for *Paul POIRET* (1879–1944), in which he distilled the designer's visual message. Such was the influence of Iribe's own designs that atelier *Madame PAQUIN* (aka Jeanne Beckers, 1869–1936, a woman who recognized a trend when she saw one) bought several of his distinctive illustrations and had them made up into outfits.

It was not just art, but also performance that inspired turn-of-the-century designers. Of huge importance and popularity was the Ballets Russes, which first performed in Paris in 1909, followed by inspired productions like Stravinsky's *Firebird* (1910). The ballet dancer Nijinsky electrified Paris in ever-more exotic outfits that took the fashion world (and umpteen groupies) by storm and his style was quickly embraced by Poiret.

**FASHION ESSENTIALS**

Leon Bakst (1866–1924) made outrageous costumes for the Ballets Russes, with a strong use of colour and oriental influence, in sharp contrast to the highly structured, boned affairs of the day. Poiret gave a ball to celebrate Ballets Russes style, but subsequently they argued as to which of them had actually created the newly popular exotic look. Whatever the truth, Bakst can be safely credited with making 'every woman determined to look like a slave in an oriental harem'. Typical examples include turbans, wide harem pants and heavily appliquéd, embroidered fabrics.

Poiret checking the bust of a new gown fits snugly (all in a day's work).

A hobble-skirted Poiret creation, c. 1915.

experiment with classically inspired clothing, including his famous Delphos gown which was a favourite of dancer Isadora Duncan (before she took the idea of floating fabrics a little bit too far).

There was also interest in ancient Greek and Cretan aesthetics: the famous scarves of *Mariano Fortuny* (1871–1949) were inspired by the discovery of Knossos in the early 1900s. Fortuny went on to

**1904** The Gibson Girl, a model of 'perfect femininity', gets Edwardian women cycling and playing tennis.

**1922** Spaniard Isaac Carasso pre-packs yoghurt with added fruit.

**1935** 'Polymer 6.6' is invented by Wallace Carothers, and later renamed nylon.

## 1900~present
# Stocking Up
### Dressing women's legs

*As accessories go, hosiery has received more than its fair share of publicity, since the days when Dr Johnson claimed they excited his 'amorous propensities'. Advertised as frequently as chocolate, washing powder or instant coffee, what women put on their legs has been big business throughout the 20th century.*

Black wool stockings were the choice of all nice girls before the First World War, white stockings being considered 'fast'.

However, by the 1920s patterned stockings were all the rage, with snakes embroidered round ankles and new colours including sky blue, flesh and yellow. Silk and artificial silk became more readily available although technical problems with the latter (it became weak when it got wet – but then what doesn't?) affected its appeal somewhat.

By the 1930s, Lastex, a rubber thread, was being used in knee-high socks and stockings although suspender belts were still seen as the safest method of attachment (and the most fun). Colours too were adventurous and diverse, with everything from copper through to sheer blue. However it was nylons that transformed the market.

How to get a leg over – advertise your wares.

Crochet as granny never intended it – worn on 1960s legs.

**1954** In New Zealand, Juliet Hulme (15) and Pauline Parker (16) murder Parker's mother with a brick wrapped in a stocking.

**1973** *Vogue* definitively declares 'a covered knee is dowdy'.

**1987** At the end of a Sicilian Mafia trial, 338 of the 452 defendants are sent to prison; 19 of them get life.

### American tan

Coco Chanel and a rich American couple called the Murphys are credited with starting the trend for soaking up rays as early as 1922. Suddenly a tan didn't scream 'Peasant!', it shouted 'Trust fund!' and with this change in attitude, black stockings were relegated to evening and funeral wear. Tan-coloured legs became the *mode du jour* and have continued to dominate the market to this day.

made even more enticing by their lack of availability during the Second World War. Soon it was possible to get them in 15 denier, which must have seemed impossibly fine at the time.

### GETTING TIGHT

The advent of the mini skirt in the 1960s heralded a gloomy time for the stocking industry, with tights deemed more suitable for exposing your thighs in (I wonder why?). But tights then suffered from the fashion for trousers, which promoted a burgeoning market in socks for women during the 1970s. At the same time, traditional, luxury silk stockings were reintroduced, the result

It's easy to keep the seams straight, so long as you stay completely still.

Sombreros and American tan tights – the obvious 1970s fashion choice.

of more effective production techniques (the ladders of success?).

By the early 1980s tights once again flirted with patterns and ankle decoration, boosted by Diana, Princess of Wales's predilection for little bows at the ankle. Colours exploded and patterns became ever more exotic, featuring animal prints, tartans, paisley pattern, checks, flower motifs and computer-generated images (for the nerds). By the 1990s hosiery was carefully tied into seasonal fashion colours and a passion for black opaque tights promoted by designers like *Rei KAWAKUBO* (b. 1942) of Comme des Garçons led full circle back to the popular black stockings of the beginning of the century *(see also pages 94–5)*.

### FASHION ESSENTIALS

When mini skirts became essential, so too did matching hosiery. Micromesh, which resembles irregular net or fishnet and lace patterns, at first small then ever larger, became the vital fabric. Mary Quant *(see pages 84–5)* produced her own line of designer hosiery as early as 1965. By 1967 she was designing floral sprig motifs and tights with her famous daisy logo (ah, sweet!).

**1917** New words that come into use this year include 'camouflage' and 'jay-walk'.

**1929** Rice Krispies are launched by Kellogg's, the cereal that is said to 'snap, crackle and pop' in the bowl.

**1939** Glasgow outlaws the playing of darts in city pubs because they are too dangerous.

1914~present

# Dressed to Kill
## Military style

*The dawn of modern warfare saw the world's armies clinging to the archaic and impractical symbols of 19th-century ceremonial dress, but there was no getting away from the change in military clothing, or the impact that it would have, in various forms, on mainstream fashion.*

### Great coats
It was in the 1950s that the army decided for the first time to let the public wear their kit and army surplus shops sprang up in major towns, especially if there was a university nearby. Duffel coats, bomber jackets, kit bags, fur-trimmed flying jackets, camouflage trousers and heavy black boots became the mainstay of impoverished students living in sub-zero apartments, long before they were restyled for the catwalks.

Girls with attitude and clunky boots adopt greatcoats in the 1990s.

Helmets became lifesavers in the First World War trenches, but British officers stubbornly continued to wear distinctive flatcaps and Sam Browne belts despite both styles being used as targets by snipers. On the other side, you couldn't get the Germans out of their spiked helmets, which they had to cover with a cloth when in battle to make them less visible. By 1915 the French army had decided to change their rather racy red trousers for a no less sartorially elegant sky blue, which unlike the more down-to-earth British khaki, was chosen to allow troops to poetically blend with the sky (provided they attacked while upside down). By 1917 the desert war also gave rise to some curious bastardizations of uniform, including khaki aprons over kilts for Scots privates and wide-brimmed hats for the newly arrived Americans.

The Second World War also saw some interesting, individual twists starting to creep in. American sailors in Hawaii dressed in white T-shirts (designed for

**1942** The US Navy pioneers the T-shirt, designed for 'greater sweat absorption' under the arms.

**1946** The first shipments of GI brides leave Southampton to be reunited with their sweethearts in the US.

**1976** Women are admitted to the US Military Academy at West Point for the first time.

maximum underarm sweat absorption) with a blue scarf, and American bomber pilots wore fur-lined jackets to protect them from unheated planes, sparking a trend that continues today. The Japanese bound their trousers to the knees and their distinctive hats (peaked and pointed with a distinctive red star) were to become an abiding image of the Second World War. Interestingly, clothing was in part

Oswald Mosley's Black Shirts in the 1930s. A look imitated ever since by suave Latin lovers out on the pull.

## FASHION ESSENTIALS

With the advent of trench warfare, troops needed clothing that hid rather than announced their presence. There are now around 350 camouflage patterns and it has become less of a protective device and more a complex symbol of war. Designs like the famous tiger stripe used in Vietnam and the quaintly named British disruptive pattern have been absorbed by street culture and appear on catwalks including that of Versace (see pages 126–7).

Baby Spice considers a new career in Her Majesty's forces.

responsible for Hitler's lack of success on the Russian front. The Soviet army, used to the cold, wrapped up in knitted caps and sheepskin coats as well as felt-lined boots, but the German uniforms, swiftly put together to keep up with Hitler's ambitious plans, proved completely inadequate to cope with the Russian winter.

### Sieg Heil!

Fascists can never resist the lure of a good uniform and the Fascist party in Italy and the Nazi party in Germany provided a plethora of militaristic examples. Even children were encouraged into uniform and the Hitler Youth wore lots of scary belts and buckles. In Britain, Oswald Mosley managed to persuade his followers into sporting black shirts, sparking a name that would stick. By the time Germany invaded Poland, the Wehrmacht was kitted out in a uniform with lightning flashes on collars, skull insignias on caps and highly polished jackboots.

The military look became popular again in 1998, featuring flak jacket body warmers and combat pants. Vintage military styling also influenced the New Romantics in the early 1980s (see pages 118–19), but in a poncy kind of way.

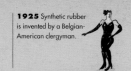

**1914** Gaston Calmette, editor of *Le Figaro*, is killed by the wife of the finance minister Joseph Caillaux, after threatening to publish some embarrassing letters.

**1921** Atlantic City comes up with a way of extending the tourist season by staging the first Miss America contest; the eight contestants represent cities, not states, and have each won a hometown popularity contest.

**1925** Synthetic rubber is invented by a Belgian-American clergyman.

## 1911~1955

# Simply Chic
## Molyneux and Balmain

*While designers like Chanel and Schiaparelli were fighting over who could come up with the most exciting detailing and the bitchiest backbite, it was left to an Irishman, Edward MOLYNEUX (1891–1974) to introduce extreme simplicity to women's fashion in the 1930s.*

Taking the new principle of freedom in dress to its logical conclusion and, with a sureness of hand that left his competitors in the shade, it was Molyneux who created the sleek and simple sheaths that epitomized the 1930s. His high-profile clients included Princess Marina of Greece

A trademark sleek black crêpe cape by Molyneux from 1947. Just the thing for supernatural glamour and spooky intrigues at the witching hour.

**STYLE ICON**
★

**Gertrude Lawrence** *(1858–1952) was the 'It' girl of the 1930s, helped by her designer of choice, Molyneux. Noel Coward wrote his comedy* Private Lives *(1930) with her in mind, and she also enthralled theatre audiences in* Lady in the Dark *(1940) and* The King and I *(1951). Regarded as one of the great comedy actresses of the time, her simple but elegant style was much copied – which must have been irritating.*

and Wallis Simpson (he designed her trousseau after she had caused a constitutional crisis in Britain by seducing the king). When Paris was occupied in 1940, he escaped to England on a coal barge, but his post-war career never reached such dizzy heights.

Molyneux favoured navy blue and black, and signature easy-to-wear, effortlessly chic, pleated skirt suits or slip-like evening dresses with the simplest detailing and colour combination. He was not above a bit of flamboyant experimentation and featured embroideries of irises and flamingos with ostrich feather trims (and who can blame him, darling?), but it is for his sultry evening pyjamas that he is perhaps best remembered.

**1934** Schiaparelli produces a 'glass dress'. A journalist remarks, 'People who live in glass dresses should not throw parties.'

**1947** French actress Martine Carol, best remembered for playing the title role in *Lola Montès*, attempts suicide by jumping off the Alma Bridge in Paris.

**1954** L. Ron Hubbard founds the Church of Scientology; he believes that man is a free spirit who can only achieve his true nature by relieving himself of the emotional burdens of the past through counselling.

## THE DRAPER'S SON

One legacy he left to the fashion world was his recognition and early employment of the designer who in many ways was to take his place. *Pierre Balmain* (1914–82). Like Molyneux, Balmain was not interested in breaking new boundaries and his collections were fêted for their wearability and cool elegance. His family was involved in the wholesale fabric business and he proved to be a good businessman, setting up his own couture house in 1945.

Pierre Balmain keeps his models happy at a 1951 show.

He went on to effectively crack the US market and design many sportswear collections. Clients included everyone from Brigitte Bardot to Marlene Dietrich, who couldn't get enough of his signature chintz shirtwaisters (to show off her incomparable legs). In the 1960s his evening dresses were made from organza with guipure lace or scattered with pale silk flowers.

### The Look

Studied simplicity was key for both designers, but eveningwear was still seen as a chance for flamboyant, but streamlined, exhibitionism. Molyneux promoted the quintessential fashion item – the little black dress (for which God bless him!) – along with dirndl skirts and bias-cut sheath dresses. Balmain loved simple day clothes and elaborately embroidered evening dresses. He couldn't resist adding mink to eveningwear, leopard to hems and ermine to collars (in those days it didn't get spray-painted in Oxford Street).

Bardot being coy in a flirty little number. Someone should tell her not to bite her nails, though.

**1904** Ice-cream dishes run out at the Louisiana Purchase Exhibition and a Syrian pastry chef rolls up his wafers into the first ice-cream cones.

**1936** Tampax introduce the first cotton tampon on a string. Early ads recommended them as being suitable for unmarried girls (i.e. virgins).

**1956** The average American teenager has $400 a year to spend on clothes, cigarettes, records and cosmetics.

1900~present

# Scents & Scentsibility
## The sweet smell of success

*While people have been rubbing their bodies with scented oils and unguents since time began (the favourite 'Eau de Woolly Mammoth' has been unavoidably discontinued), the mass production of designer perfumes and scents is a very 20th-century concept and, like everything else, relies on creating the right 'image'.*

Surreal advertising sells 'Shocking' to adventurous 1930s women.

### FASHION ESSENTIALS

The legendary Chanel No. 5 was created by Ernest Beaux for Chanel and first marketed in 1921 in a bottle designed by French artist Sem. It contains 130 ingredients with a fresh and floral top note of ylang ylang and neroli, while the heart is blended jasmine and rose with a woody base of sandalwood and vetiver. It became notorious when Marilyn Monroe declared that No. 5 was the only thing she wore in bed. Famous faces from past No. 5 campaigns include Lauren Hutton, Catherine Deneuve, Jean Shrimpton and Carol Bouquet. Chanel told women that they should wear perfume wherever they want to be kissed – I presume she meant unless it stings!

Le classique du genre.

In 1900, the great perfume houses such as Yardley and House of Coty ruled the air waves. However it didn't take long for fashion designers to work out that perfume was a great way to promote their collections, so the designer perfume was born. One of the first to leap on the bandwagon was Coco Chanel *(see pages 42–3)*, along with *Jeanne* LANVIN (1867–1946), but before long they were joined by *Jean* PATOU (1880–1936), *Edward* MOLYNEUX (1891–1974), Worth *(see pages 12–13)* and Schiaparelli *(see pages 44–5)*. Schiaparelli's 'Shocking', with its wild torso bottle, and Chanel's more sober and classic Chanel No. 5 slugged it out on the shelves. By 1940 things had become very oriental with experiments in heavy, exotic perfumes

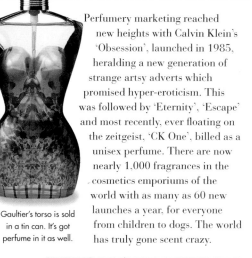

like 'Joy' from Patou. Post-war, fresher and lighter fragrances were launched by *Pierre Balmain* (1914–82) with 'Vent Vert' and Christian Dior *(see page 70)* with 'Miss Dior'.

Cult perfumes of the 1960s included 'Arpège' by Lanvin and 'Calèche' from Hermès, while in the 1970s Yves Saint Laurent rediscovered the Orient with his super-popular 'Opium', which could be smelled up to a mile away (especially by the Drug Enforcement Agency). Things started to get silly in the 1980s with the dubiously named and bottled 'Poison', which started a trend for sickly floral scents. Jean-Paul Gaultier camped up the torso design of 'Shocking' with a pink corset container, as well as introducing a men's perfume clothed in tight striped T-shirt.

Gaultier's torso is sold in a tin can. It's got perfume in it as well.

Perfumery marketing reached new heights with Calvin Klein's 'Obsession', launched in 1985, heralding a new generation of strange artsy adverts which promised hyper-eroticism. This was followed by 'Eternity', 'Escape' and most recently, ever floating on the zeitgeist, 'CK One', billed as a unisex perfume. There are now nearly 1,000 fragrances in the cosmetics emporiums of the world with as many as 60 new launches a year, for everyone from children to dogs. The world has truly gone scent crazy.

### Perfumes for Men

Men used to be severely limited when it came to fragrances and the perfume industry has worked hard at making it macho to smell nice. After years of choosing between Old Spice and Brut, men now have a bewildering choice of perfumes or, the preferred title, 'men's fragrances' to choose from. Most of the big houses, including Calvin Klein, Jil Sander and Jean-Paul Gaultier, have dedicated men's fragrances, while new scents by Hugo Boss and Tommy Hilfiger are capturing the younger market. Advertising, too, is more targeted, witness 'Opium pour Homme' by Yves Saint Laurent featuring actor Rupert Everett reclining in a satin dressing gown to sell its image.

Kate Moss sprawls naked (except for her Obsession of course) across a billboard on Sunset Strip.

**1918** Miss Margaret Owen sets a typing speed record of 170 words per minute.

**1930** Marlene Dietrich plays a callous dancehall singer called Lola in *The Blue Angel*.

**1965** French rock stars Johnny Haliday and Sylvie Vartan get married.

1914~present

# Lend Us A Lens
## Fashion photographers

*Fashion photographers do more than just snap a few frocks (or so they tell us). They spread the word about new styles and in many cases they have been responsible for setting trends, working closely with designers. As Irving PENN (b. 1917) put it, they are responsible for 'selling dreams not clothes'.*

Man Ray works up a few sketches toward another fashion dreamscape.

### Snappy women

Key women photographers have included the Surrealist influenced Lee Miller (1907–77), who posed in Hitler's bath in 1945, Louise Dahl-Wolfe (1895–1989), who pioneered the healthy outdoor girl look (pah!) and was one of the first to work with natural light, Genevieve with her love of unusual backgrounds, the disturbing and emotionally raw work of Diane Arbus (1923–71) and Corrine Day, whose grungy realism helped to launch the model Kate Moss's career as a highly paid stick insect.

Gradually replacing sketches on the pages of *Vogue* and other glossies, the first fashion photographers were true pioneers. *Edward STEICHEN* (1879–1973) was taking pictures of Poiret's collection as early as 1911 while *Baron Adolphe DE MEYER* (1868–1949) was the first photographer contracted to *Vogue* in 1914. In the 1930s Surrealist *Man RAY* (1890–1976) worked with *George HOYNINGEN-HUENE* (1900–68) to produce images that experimented with geometry, light and shade, and *Horst P. HORST* (b. 1906) introduced spotlights to highlight details of the dress and played with elaborate backgrounds.

The New Look *(see pages 70–1)* called for a new form of photography, that was elegant and aloof. *Irving PENN* (b. 1917) gave a formal, almost sculptural dignity to his aristocratic-looking models and still-life compositions (most notably in his famous marketing campaigns for Clinique). *Richard AVEDON* (b. 1923), with his wide-angle lens and strange camera

**1968** Kodak launches the Instamatic camera, with two lens settings – cloudy and sunny.

**1972** The world is horrified by a picture of a young Vietnamese girl running in terror after being hit by napalm, during the Vietnam War.

**1992** Newspaper photos appear of Sarah, the Duchess of York, having her toes sucked by her 'financial adviser' John Bryan.

angles, added a distinctive edgy dimension, setting his models in unfamiliar territory.

In the 1970s fashion photographers became media celebrities, following the lead of *David BAILEY* (b. 1938) with his string of high-profile model girlfriends (and wives). The aggressive sexuality in photos by *Helmut NEWTON* (b. 1920) proved a perfect medium for the fashions of the 1980s and *Steven MEISEL* (b. 1954) has to take much responsibility for the flourishing cult of the supermodel *(see pages 132–3)* but by the end of the decade anti-fashion statements were becoming popular with the grunge-influenced work of *Jürgen TELLER* (b. 1964). In the late 1990s a new style labelled 'heroin chic', using bare-faced, seemingly stoned models, was widely criticised for glamorizing addiction.

David Bailey marries Catherine Deneuve in 1965. The film *Blow-Up* glorified his high-profile love life.

## STYLE ICON ★

*Despite an uneasy relationship with fashion photography,* **Cecil Beaton** *(1904-80) kept returning to the medium throughout his career. Although limited by the magazine restrictions of the time he experimented with images culled from Salvador Dali as well as flirting with Rococo themes. He managed to take some grittier pictures during the war, shooting models in bombed-out houses, but by 1955 he had established himself in a comfortable rut, playing with neo-Edwardian styles. Fashion bored him until the 1960s when, inspired by the new era (and possibly by the fact that the models looked like boys), he came out of semi-retirement to snap Twiggy and Jean Shrimpton.*

Restrained and stylized elegance was Beaton's trademark style, as in this artsy shot from 1948—kind of Jane Austen chic you might call it.

**1922** The Asian game of mah-jongg becomes all the rage with American women, who dress in kimonos and drink exotic teas while playing.

**1925** 'Pretty Boy' Floyd robs a post office in St Louis of $350, beginning his 9-year career in which he will rob more than 30 banks in the Midwest.

**1928** A Board of Health commissioner stops the Madison Square Garden Dance marathon in its 428th hour after one contestant has collapsed vomiting blood and been taken to hospital.

## 1920s~1930s
# Fads and Flappers
## The Roaring Twenties

*Imagine being a beauty prior to the First World War and emerging on the other side a monster. This was the fate of many women entering the 1920s, whose rosy cheeks and plump bosoms no longer conformed to society's idea of beauty. Instead, it was considered chic to have the body of a fifteen-year-old boy and a deep tan, preferably gained on the Riviera or from a new-fangled sunbed that would probably give you more than just a golden glow.*

Sudden flesh exposure: not many years earlier, it was considered shocking to show an ankle.

For this was the era of 'bright young things' who smoked furiously, drank cocktails and danced the Charleston to one of the latest jazz tunes. The flapper voted, she worked, she drove: by the end of the decade there were 23 million cars on the roads in the US, and often, when descending from her Hispano-Suiza after a night on the town, she flashed her legs in flesh-coloured rayon stockings. Her silhouette changed too. By the mid-decade, bustles and leg o'mutton sleeves were only worn by matriachs and maiden aunts, while the rest of society adopted the short, slim, drop-waisted dress that had been popularized by Chanel *(see pages 42–3)*. Lesbian chic was born in the wake of Radclyffe Hall's sensational novel *The Well of Loneliness* (1928), and women of all persuasions raided their husbands' wardrobes for ties, scarves and pyjamas.

Men retaliated by wearing voluminous Oxford Bags, trousers with legs as much as two

The 'dance till you drop' society captured in a *Punch* cartoon.

**1930** Ethel Merman (Zimmermann) quits her $35-a-week secretarial job for a $350-a-week role in the Gershwin musical *Girl Crazy*.

**1933** James Hilton writes a novel, *The Lost World*, about a place called Shangri-la in the Himalayas. More than sixty years later, explorers are still trying to find it.

**1937** US spinach growers erect a statue of Popeye, in honour of his services to their industry.

feet wide and, as a golfing craze swept the continent, plus fours and Argyle-patterned sweaters were considered simply 'top hole'.

As hemlines rose, so too did levels of tolerance. Tennis ace and queen of Wimbledon, Suzanne Lenglen was dressed in a radical new silhouette by *Jean* PATOU (1880–1936), that revolutionized subsequent women's sportswear with its shorter proportions. On the beach, skimpy new swimsuits eradicated tan-lines (important with all those backless evening-dresses) and a more extreme healthy lifestyle was advocated. Elderly British Queen Mary reportedly averted her eyes in embarrassment when confronted by the scantily clad chorus at the musical hit *No No, Nanette* that rocked the London stage. The permissive society had arrived.

Suddenly, amid the hilarity, on 29 October 1929 came the Wall Street Crash and with it an economic disaster that famously resulted in suicides, bankruptcies and nearly 10 million unemployed. The champagne bubble had burst but if it hadn't been for the fashions of the Roaring Twenties, we might still be wearing corsets.

**Trivial pursuits**

Many fads were popularized in the Twenties, including pogo sticks, crossword puzzles, yo-yos, mah jongg and bridge – and one million packets of potato crisps were sold in 1928 when they were first introduced. Dieting and health cures were all the rage, helping women to achieve the regulation boyish silhouette, and the craze for naturism enabled them to show off those sleek new figures to the full.

### STYLE ICON
### ★

*Combining graceful barefoot movements, flowing Grecian costumes and maverick views on everything from ballet to marriage, San Francisco native* **Isadora Duncan** *(1878–1927) is rightly remembered as one of the pioneers of modern dance. Though she achieved international fame, she was the subject of continual controversy, not only because of her opinion that dance was more natural when conducted bare-legged in a flimsy shift, but also because she insisted on remaining a 'free' woman and had two children out of wedlock. Sadly her life was dogged by tragedy: her children drowned in a car accident, and she was later strangled to death when her trademark flowing scarf became tangled in the wheels of an open sports car in which she was riding.*

The statuesque Isadora Duncan in characteristic Classical garb.

**1922** Flappers bind their breasts in an attempt to achieve a boyish silhouette.

**1943** Howard Hughes designs a cantilevered bra to display Jane Russell's cleavage to best effect in *The Outlaws*. She says it is very uncomfortable.

**1948** According to the Kinsey Report, 56 percent of US men have been unfaithful to their partners.

1920~Present

# Bra-Vo

## Their cups runneth over

Flat-chested flappers.

*After the First World War, skirts got shorter and narrower, hips disappeared and busts had to be flat, yet the flapper still needed to be able to dance the night away. A serious rethink was needed in the underwear department.*

### Designer undies

Calvin Klein started a trend for affordable designer-label underwear promoted through assiduous use of models such as the rap singer Marky Mark. A strange trend developed for wearing underwear poking out of trousers (or over them if you were a superhero). Big designer names like Dolce & Gabbana, Prada and Donna Karan followed, flooding the market. Having a designer's name close to the skin became as important as having an Armani suit, although loose licensing and easy availability saw the kudos of designer underwear diminish in the 1990s.

It was now that the bra came into its own and started being taken seriously by manufacturers, ironically to minimize rather than maximize the bust and give that desirable boyish figure. Firm corsets were used to iron out curvy figures and elastic was slowly transforming the fabric of underwear. Cami-knickers enjoyed a surge of popularity and by the 1930s a more natural feel was creeping in to

women's underwear (but fortunately he was arrested). Camisoles started to replace corsets, while artificial fabrics such as rayon emerged as a viable alternative to silk, crêpe de chine and satin, making slinky underwear available to the masses.

Singer Dale Bozzio makes good use of the tin-foil cartons her lunch was delivered in.

Strapless bras were introduced in 1938 to suit the trend for backless dresses.

**1971** On the French Riviera, police order topless women sunbathers to cover up.

**1988** Journalist Anna Quindlen claims 'If men g pregnant, there would be safe, reliable methods of birth control. They'd be inexpensive, too.'

**1996** The survival rate for cancer is 40%; in 1920, it was less than 20%.

More comfort-conscious underwear came into fashion, including the new look corset, known as a 'roll on with built in suspenders' (and I thought that was a kind of cross-Channel ferry!).

The New Look *(see pages 70–1)* brought with it the 'waspie', a short corset usually worn over a roll-on or light pantie girdle. The new generation of sweater girls meant an emphasis on bosoms, which became scarily sharp points, stiffened and built up to frightening proportions. Flaring petticoats attached to strapless bra corsets were standard for creating the kind of bulk needed for extravagant 1950s eveningwear.

Women gradually moved towards a more natural silhouette with the invention of Spandex and Elastane, the youth revolution of the 1960s, and the emergence of women's libbers declaring that bras were

combinations, and moulded bras got rid of the tricky problem of seams showing through thin T-shirts. In the 1990s, women began to hanker after something a little bit special and the lingerie market exploded in a plethora of lace, leopard-skin prints and feather-trimmed satin.

Designer underwear makes its Marky Mark.

---

### FASHION ESSENTIALS

Despite all the lip service paid to the natural silhouette, it seems what women really want is a cleavage. Witness the long and successful career of the Wonderbra, introduced by Gossard in 1969 and said to be the top-selling bra in the world. Repackaged by Playtex in the 1990s and given lots of media attention, the Wonderbra remains *the* underwear essential. Hello boys, indeed!

---

symbols of male oppression. Mini skirts brought a new fashion for knickers with bright patterns and colours that were worn to be seen. The girdle was gradually phased out and replaced with bra and brief

**1909** Japanese novelist Ogai Mori writes *Vita Sexualis*, combatting the notion that men have no control over their sexual urges.

**1934** A statute in Austria bans anyone from making jokes about the short stature of Chancellor Dollfuss.

**1953** Fifth Avenue's double-decker buses, called Queen Marys, go out of service.

**1966** Nancy Sinatra's single 'These Boots are Made for Walkin" sells almost 4 million copies and associates her forever with the white vinyl, mid-calf Go-Go boot.

1900s~present

# Step Out in Style

## These boots *weren't* made for walking

*The notion of footwear was born when the first caveman bound his feet with scraps of animal skin, but it was only in the early years of the 20th century that shoes became a fast-changing fashion staple, as the high-laced 'granny boot' of the 19th century was relegated to the elderly or infirm and rising hemlines put feet on display.*

Brocade evening shoes with diamanté decoration, Paris 1924.

The real boom in fashion footwear began in the early 1920s as shoes were mass-manufactured, enabling women to buy styles to suit the numerous changes of dress that were required during the day. Buckles and trims reigned supreme, as did sequinned straps and all manner of flouncy fabrications. In the 1930s shoes became chunkier with wedged soles, and in the 1950s, when women were desperate to move away from the chunky utilitarian styles of the post-war years, they opted for simple, spindly styles culminating in the vertiginously high stiletto, which was responsible for ruining more floors than a swarm of termites.

During the 1960s, footwear became more frivolous. Parisian designer *André Courrèges* (b. 1923) introduced flat-soled boots to complement his simple shifts and

### FASHION ESSENTIALS

The Nike swoosh was inspired by the Greek goddess Nike (the winged goddess of victory) and was designed in 1971 by Caroline Davidson, a graphics student at Portland State University. She was paid a measly $35 to create the world-famous logo that, twenty years later would generate an annual income of over $4 billion for the company. As they say, 'Just do it!'

Another platform casualty; broken ankles were common.

the hippies *(see pages 100–1)* of the late decade introduced psychedelic-printed styles embroidered with all manner of motifs. In the early 1970s the platform reigned supreme, so much so that by the mid-decade it was normal for even the most conventional parent to sport a two-inch heel: some styles made orthopaedic footwear look delicate in comparison.

After this, as fashion reinvented trends from earlier in the century, the period being revived dictated the look of the shoe. However, running parallel (literally) with the birth of the fitness craze of the mid 1980s, the growing popularity of rap and R'n'B music in the US made the trainer or sneaker a high-fashion item. In extreme circumstances, trainers provoked cases of 'taxing', where those wearing the latest styles were mugged and sometimes killed for the sake of the right brand.

By the 1990s, footwear fashions were dominated by the Italian brands Prada and Gucci *(see pages 128–9)* and *Manolo BLAHNIK* (b. 1943), whose vertiginous high heels are affectionately known as Manolos.

## The high life

While today's 'lady of the night' tends to wear stilettos, the 16th-century choice was the *chopine*, a platform overshoe that could reach up to 30 inches high. *Chopines* were worn by wealthy Venetian women, who often required servants to support their perilous passage along the quay-sides, but were also popular with prostitutes plying their trade on the canal banks, because they kept them clear of the rats and sewage. So if you think the Spice Girls were the first to lend sex appeal to the platform, think again – Venetian Spice used to make a good living from them as well.

Chunky but funky: the Spice Girls relaunch platform trainers, courtesy of makers Buffalo.

For the more ergonomically minded, shoes became ugly but comfortable in the guise of Birkenstock sandals. Today there is no footwear style that personifies the age. Footwear choices are as much to do with the personality of the wearer as they are connected to any prevailing fashion trend. From patent leather fetish boots with multiple zips and straps to Prada Sport sneakers with a discreet red flash at the heel or the latest techno trainer, in the late 1990s anything goes – except bunions.

**1921** In Chicago, women are fined for wearing short skirts and having bare arms.

**1929** Edwin Hubble shows that the nebulae of the Milky Way are speeding away, leading others to believe that the universe is expanding (he doesn't agree).

**1934** Cole Porter's 'I Get a Kick out of You' is the first popular song to mention drug-taking – in this case cocaine.

1920s~present

# Baubles and Bitterness
## Coco Chanel

Coco in 1931, thinking up her next bitchy *bon mot.*

*She may be remembered as the greatest designer of the 20th century. She may have taken jersey from the domain of men's underwear and transformed it into pared-down luxury sportswear. She may have been the first designer to take elements of menswear and adapt them for the womenswear market. She may have created the first fragrance to receive worldwide acclaim. But despite these accolades, Gabrielle 'Coco' CHANEL (1883–1971) was a racist, homophobic Nazi sympathizer whose extraordinary talent for design was matched by a notoriously unpleasant personality.*

**B**orn poor and illegitimate, Chanel's talent for weaving untruth and mythology began early in her life. She adopted the name 'Coco' during an abortive career as a café singer, before finding the role of courtesan more profitable. One of her lovers helped to fund the opening of a small boutique in Deauville in 1913, where she introduced her

Audrey Hepburn wears a little black dress for *Breakfast at Tiffany's.*

### FASHION ESSENTIALS

To achieve the Chanel look, opt for braid-trimmed tweed suits with collarless boxy jackets; the jersey twin-set; rows of artificial pearls and gilt chains; quilted handbags on gilt chains; sling-backs or two-tone shoes; gilt buttons on blazers; menswear adopted as womenswear; and, of course, the little black dress. Colours should be grey, black, navy blue or beige. We haf ways of making you obey!

signature jersey pieces at prices that could run into hundreds of pounds for even the simplest styles. In 1916, American *Vogue* declared that Chanel's simple yet discreetly expensive gowns were 'synonymous with chic', and her influence began in earnest.

**1952** Salvador Dali writes in his diary, 'There is only one difference between a madman and me. I am not mad.'

**1976** Audrey Hepburn makes *Robin and Marian* with Sean Connery, her first movie for nine years.

**1995** Three men steal gems worth FF 250 million (about £30 million) from the Carlton Hotel, Cannes.

The Chanel silhouette personified the 1920s. Her famous 'little black dress' of 1926 was described by American *Vogue* as a 'fashion Ford' and her own slim and elegant appearance made her the best possible advertisement for the quintessentially modern clothes. Her radical break from the prevailing opulence made her contemporaries seem terribly demodé. Of Poiret *(see page 24)*, the reigning couturier in Paris, she said 'his eccentricity is dying', professing to find his style and colours 'barbaric' and opting herself for simple lines and a palette that was predominantly beige and black.

A decade later, she was eclipsed by Elsa Schiaparelli *(see pages 44–5)* and the long, romantic dresses that she had professed to despise became part of her style. Her couture house closed in 1939 at the outbreak of war and didn't reopen until 1954, when she was 71 years old. Then her

The Paris salon closed from 1939 till 1954 because of her ill-judged wartime pursuits.

true sense of style – the boxy suit, the strings of imitation jewellery and the brightly trimmed tweeds – provided a welcome antidote to Dior's New Look *(see pages 78–1)*, with its billowing skirts and nipped-in waists. By the 1960s Chanel had become synonymous with bourgeois chic and her shadowy lifestyle had been romanticized by biographers.

After her death, the house of Chanel became a fashion dinosaur, catering solely for the rich and elderly, until, in 1983, the company's fortunes were once again revived by the appointment of Karl Lagerfeld *(see pages 78–9)*, who rests incumbent today. His timing couldn't have been better. Fashion during the 1980s was obsessed with aggressive ostentation, and his subversion of the classically chic two-piece suit and ropes of pearls and gilt chains fitted the mood. Denim mini-skirts, Chanel-logoed underwear and quilted bags designed to hold mobile phones and Evian bottles were all great successes. Coco may have been spinning in her grave, but the public lapped it up.

### Fashion's fascist

According to a recently de-classified British intelligence archive, Chanel was denounced as a German agent as early as 1943, when she took part in a campaign to influence her former lover the Duke of Westminster's old friend Sir Winston Churchill. In April 1944, just before Germany collapsed, Chanel travelled to Berlin to meet some high Nazi functionaries. When she was arrested by Allied forces after the liberation of Paris she explained the fact that she'd had a Nazi officer lover by saying 'At my age when a man wants to sleep with me [she was 62], one doesn't ask to see his passport.' She was soon released, probably to prevent her revealing incriminating information about all her high-born British chums who had been cozy with the Nazis.

**1922** In Denver, a police car called a 'bandit chaser' is introduced, using a Cadillac engine.

**1929** Cocteau writes *Les Enfants Terribles* about a claustrophic brother and sister who live together in a single room.

**1930** American astronomer Clyde William Tombaugh finds Pluto, the ninth planet from the Sun; it is only about two-thirds of the size of Earth's Moon.

## 1922~1939
# Is This Some Kind of Joke?
### Elsa Schiaparelli

Mixing your metaphors.

*Imagine a hat as a lamb chop, a necklace fashioned out of a string of aspirins or a costly evening dress printed with trompe l'oeil tear motifs. All were designed by the maverick Italian designer Elsa SCHIAPARELLI (1890–1973), whose alliance with the Surrealist movement created some of fashion's best visual jokes and popularized a radical fusion between art and fashion that had as much impact in the 1930s as the Punk movement and Vivienne Westwood did in the late 1970s.*

Madame Schiaparelli: a Surrealist with savvy.

Schiaparelli arrived in Paris in 1922 to play the role of impoverished aristocrat and cultural guide to wealthy American women. One day, while leading a shopping tour at Poiret's maison de couture *(see page 24),* she impulsively tried on a magnificent evening coat. Poiret offered to give her the ensemble and encouraged her to design clothes herself. In many ways Shiap (as she was affectionately known) took over where Poiret left off: she inherited his love of rich, opulent colours and fabrics, and added a wealth of traditionally feminine ornamentation and fantasy fuelled by her love of theatre and the exotic – and, let's face it, a weird sense of humour.

The mainstay of Schiaparelli's early career was the broad-shouldered suit she designed in 1931, which prompted numerous imitations after the silhouette was copied by droves of Hollywood celebs *(see pages 54–5).*

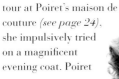

Marlene Dietrich in her big-shouldered Schiaparelli suit.

**1931** Alka-Seltzer, the hangover cure of choice, is introduced with a 'plink! plink! fizz!'.

**1934** Dorothy Parker quips that 'Brevity is the soul of lingerie.'

**1939** Clark Gable marries Carole Lombard and Tyrone Power marries a French actress called Annabella, whom he's only known for a few months.

She produced countless severely tailored suits (launching the shoulder pad) and little black dresses for members of the haute bourgeoisie, but is best remembered for her creative liaisons with the Surrealist movement, most notably with *Jean Cocteau* (1889–1963) and *Salvador Dalí* (1904–89). With Cocteau she made a jacket with embroidered hands that clasped the wearer's torso; with Dalí, the famous 'tear' print and a number of witty and outrageous hats that culminated in the ultimate Surrealist accessory – an upside-down shoe perched on the head. Wealthy society loved the ingenuity of such pieces and her most outré creations were given the seal of approval by fashion leaders such as the Duchess of Windsor

## Jealous? Who, moi?

Irked by her rival's success and enraged by her admittance to the upper echelons of society she could not penetrate, Coco Chanel disparagingly referred to Schiaparelli as 'that Italian artist who makes clothes'. Mainbocher *(see page 57)* complained bitterly about the amount of coverage her clothes received in French *Vogue*. Some people just don't seem to have a sense of humour.

*(see page 57)* who wore her evening dress featuring a giant lobster garnished with parsley. Ultimately Schiaparelli was so successful because her boldness was teamed with considerable commercial savvy. She was, as Cocteau pointed out, the dressmaker of eccentricity: 'She knows how to go too far,' he claimed. At the outbreak of the Second World War, she closed her business and fled to the US, and never regained her influence in the post-war period.

### FASHION ESSENTIALS

To achieve the Schiaparelli look, choose a simple basic silhouette and add your own witty trimmings: sharp suits with shoulder pads combined with trompe l'oeil effects, such as her black sweater with a white bow knitted into it; padlocks, insects, lips, acrobats, soldiers or zodiac signs on clothes or costume jewellery; scarves covered in newsprint; prominent zips and wacky buttons in the shape of peanuts or bumble bees; Tyrolean hats. Wear her 'Shocking' perfume *(see pages 32–3)* in the torso bottle designed by Leonor Fini and the colour 'shocking pink', which was named by her.

The Duchess of Windsor's famous lobster dress (though that's not the Duchess of Windsor inside it).

**1906** The nickelodeon (where you see a moving picture projected onto a screen for a nickel) is introduced; there will be 10,000 in the US within three years.

**1926** The cloche pulled over one eye is in fashion, 'To show a forehead would have caused a scandal. Chic starts at the eyebrows.'

**1933** In the US, a Stetson hat costs $5 and a gas stove is $23.95.

1900~present

# Fashion Headlines

## From pillboxes to baseball caps

The Mad Hatter's tea party? No, a 1946 ad for turbans.

*At the beginning of the twentieth century, being seen without a hat was tantamount to shouting 'I'm a floozy' and, just to be on the safe side, hats were often worn indoors and out. Now, with brief exceptions (Princess Diana's penchant for little tricornes prompted a flurry of millinery purchases), hats are consigned to special occasions and for keeping out the cold.*

Early in the century, hat styles kept up a fast and furious pace, changing from impossibly wide-brimmed *My Fair Lady* affairs to sultry curled turbans. Flowers, stuffed birds, baskets of fruits – there was no end to what could be piled on top of a pre-war hat. By the First World War hats went upwards rather than outwards: the cloche was introduced in 1917 and continued to dominate the 1920s, although wide soft brims were also popular, as were toques, berets and boaters. By the 1930s Surrealism and hats had become intertwined, thanks in part to Elsa Schiaparelli *(see pages 44-5)*. Fantasy was the order of the day with turbans, tricornes, coup-de-vent hats and even hats made to resemble shoes (giving a new meaning to standing on your head?).

The Second World War brought the world of millinery up short with Utility styles leaving little room for creativity, even in the United States, where hats actually shrunk in size. However in 1947 the New Look *(see pages 70–1)* saw the introduction of modified coolie hats. Boaters returned along with berets, and materials included felt, straw, taffeta and flannel, trimmed with brightly coloured feathers.

VOGUE

The Black and White Idea

London Season

An Irving Penn shot for *Vogue*, 1950. Fine so long as you don't try to eat or drink.

**1939** Eugen Weidmann is the last person to be publicly guillotined in France.

**1964** Julie Andrews and Dick Van Dyke wear fetching straw boaters for the film *Mary Poppins*.

**1988** David Shilling is famous for his outrageous hats; his mother has to wear ever more ostentatious examples to Royal Ascot each year.

### Master Milliners

Jean Barthet (b. 1930) – designs for Montana, Sonia Rykiel and Ungaro; signature styles include highly structured creations and scaled-down fedoras. Lilly Daché (1904–89) – best known for her draped turbans, snoods and cloche hats. Stephen Jones (b.1957) – has worked for Gaultier, Hamnett and Westwood; signature designs are outrageous and sculptural; worn by Madonna and Boy George. Philip Treacy (b. 1967) – works with Karl Lagerfeld and John Galliano; outstanding dramatic hats, often featuring feathers and sculptural forms.

The large picture hats of the 1950s were much photographed and crowns became wider and wider until Jackie Kennedy turned fashion on its head by adopting little pillboxes. Edwardian nostalgia also swept the board with veils and fabric linings.

The cultural imperative was waning and headgear was soon relegated to formal events or for practical necessities (like bad hair days). The 1960s brought mass-produced hats with a more casual feel and a reintroduction of the cloche for the Biba look. The smash-hit *Four Weddings and a Funeral* (1994) did much to encourage hat wearing at weddings, and baseball caps and woolly Kangol hats were adopted by 1990s pop stars. However, whatever your mother says, the dominance of the hat is dead – wherever you go, bare heads are the norm.

Julia Roberts cunningly disguised as Che Guevara in the 1999 film *Notting Hill*.

Andie McDowell's black straw by Herald & Heart in *Four Weddings*.

## STYLE ICON
★

*Hat enthusiasts and trend-setters have included Jackie Kennedy in her tiny pill-boxes; Princess Diana in her feather-trimmed tricornes; the Queen Mum in her tipsy little old lady picture hats; Boy George in his barmitzvah boy hats; Jay Kay of Jamiroquai in his exaggerated Mad Hatter number; the British banker and his bowler; Audrey Hepburn in Cecil Beaton's extravaganza homage to Edwardiana,*

*My Fair Lady; Sean Connery as early James Bond in quintessential 1960s trilby; Peter Sellers in his deerstalker; Diane Keaton cute in floppy hat as Annie Hall.*

**1930** Jack & Charlie's 21 Club opens in New York. If they are raided by Prohibition officers, they push a button that tips all the alcohol off the shelves and down a chute to the cellar.

**1933** Richard Hollingshead of New Jersey is granted a patent for a 'ramp drive-in system' and opens his first public drive-in cinema.

**1941** The Grand Coulee Dam on the Mississippi River is the world's largest hydroelectric plant.

1927~1960

# Synthetic Style
## Nylon shirts and Crimplene pants

*After centuries of relying on the old staples of wool, silk and cotton, the brave new world of the 20th century turned its attention to artificial fibres. What were needed were new über fabrics, capable of drying fast, keeping their shape and above all cheap enough to meet the fashion demands of the masses. Scientists got to work, and quickly came up with the goods!*

Wrap up warm in Du Pont's pink Orlon coat (1954 model).

### Artificial acumen

Two giants of the synthetic industry, the British Courtaulds and American company Du Pont have both made considerable contributions to the development of synthetic fibres this century. Courtaulds smartly cornered the market on viscose yarn production in the UK and America, and also made artificial silk or rayon before developing the first British acrylic fibre, Courtelle. Du Pont, based in Delaware, started life as a gunpowder manufacturer before moving into synthetic manufacture with first cellophane, then rayon and later nylon and Corfam, one of the first ever leather substitutes.

O By the 1950s there was a huge enthusiasm for all things man-made, following the massive breakthroughs made with synthetics based on or oil products. This new gener of fibres, including rayon, nylo tricels and acrylic, were held u as the answer to all clothing problems, easy to wash (they had to be, because they made you sweat more!), easy to look after, cheap and perfect for fashion styling (even if they made your hair stand on end).

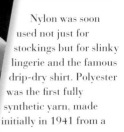

Nylon was soon used not just for stockings but for slinky lingerie and the famous drip-dry shirt. Polyester was the first fully synthetic yarn, made initially in 1941 from a

Mary Quant's mini-skimmy in Carnaby green Courtelle.

**1947** The first Edinburgh Festival takes place. Several groups arrive uninvited and perform in church halls and other venues, and thus the Festival Fringe is born.

**1953** Women are impregnated with frozen sperm in Ohio.

**1956** Swiss engineer Georges de Mertral invents Velcro. Its name comes from the French *velours* (velvet) and crochet.

For any occasion, you can't go wrong in a nylon twin-set and Terylene skirt.

petrol base and developed in the 1940s then instantly utilized by manufacturers who heralded its easy-care properties. Terylene was used for pleated dresses that never dropped a pleat, while acrylic will be forever associated with sweaters that were practically indestructible (despite desperate attempts by the Style Police). Imaginative variations on these fibres included Crimplene (much used for trousers), Dacron, Acrilan, Courtelle (which didn't stretch or shrink), Orlon (used as a substitute for wool) and Dralon.

However, the idea of science as the answer to all our problems started to turn sour, as ecological movements highlighted the unsustainable damage being done to the planet. Man-made fabrics were an early casualty, not helped by the fact that scientists hadn't entirely ironed out certain problems. Acrylics didn't have the same warmth as wool and were inclined to stretch and pill; other fibres caused static and electric shocks, or wouldn't let the skin breath. The backlash was to last until the 1980s when modified fibres like Lycra and Tencel were introduced.

## FASHION ESSENTIALS

Believe it or not, nylon and polyester were the sexiest fibres around in the 1950s. Nylon came first, invented in 1927 by Dr Wallace H. Carothers for Du Pont. He managed to find a way to create a fibre using synthetic long-chain polymers, to instant success. The backlash against nylon clothing started when it was discovered that garments were not breathable and resembled portable saunas in summer. Polyester was a later arrival on the scene, invented by J.F. Winfield and J.T. Dickson of the Calico Printer's Association. What they created was a fibre composed of ethylene glycol and terephthalic acid. Polyester became a fabric staple and continues to be much used in clothing manufacture, not least because of its easy care, quick drying, easy wear properties.

Crease-resistant, shrink-resistant Orlon, the answer to 1950s-girls' prayers.

**1934** Car designer Ferdinand Porsche designs the Volkswagen Beetle.

**1939** General Franco's Nationalist forces win the Spanish Civil War; half a million Spaniards died , more being executed than perishing in battle.

**1944** In the film *Lady in the Dark*, Ginger Rogers's mink and sequins costume, made by Edith Head, costs $35,000.

## 1930~1968

# Fashion's Picasso

### Balenciaga

*Cristobal BALENCIAGA (1895-1972) is without doubt the best-known Spanish designer of the century. Christened 'fashion's Picasso' by Cecil Beaton (see page 35), he was also a consummate technician whose clothes were worn by screen divas Ava Gardner and Ingrid Bergman, as well as Fabiola, Queen of Belgium.*

Ava Gardner's stunning figure was often accentuated by Balenciaga's superb cut.

Before you wear the outfit (1955 design), first practise the funny walk.

He trained as a tailor and set up dressmaking establishments in San Sebastian and Madrid before making his mark in Paris by opening the house of Balenciaga in 1937, which he ran for 31 years till his retirement in 1968. Obsessive about privacy, he sensibly left it to the people around him to wax lyrical about his clothing. Even his old adversary Coco Chanel (never a woman to hold back on bitchy criticism) grudgingly admired Balenciaga, saying 'Only he is capable of cutting material, assembling a creation and sewing it by hand. The others are simply fashion designers.' In other words, a regular Mr Do-it-All.

It was this cutting skill combined with an almost obsessive need to control every stage of production that made Balenciaga such a fashion icon (although presumably

### FASHION ESSENTIALS

Like Balenciaga, French couturier Madeleine Vionnet (1876–1975) was more interested in perfecting cut than unnecessary ornamentation. Her development of the bias cut, where fabrics were cut against the grain of the weave, brought a new sinuosity to fashion, gently emphasizing the curve of the body without unflattering cling. Many current designs show her influence.

**1947** Multimillionaire matador Manuel Rodriguez (Manolete) is fatally gored during a bullfight in Linares.

**1955** Spanish-born Severo Ochoa synthesizes RNA in a laboratory, bringing the day closer when it will be possible to create life from inert materials.

**1968** The makeup look this year is pale skin, baby pink rouge, shiny plum lips and smoky eyes. The page-boy haircut is introduced.

not such a wonderful boss). He was involved in every stage, from producing sketches, choosing, cutting and sewing fabrics, even deciding on matching accessories and training his mannequins (walk, pose, smile, giggle, light a cigarette – what else do mannequins do?). He is credited with improving 19th-century cutting techniques and was never afraid to experiment, reaching new heights with his one-seam coat in 1961 *(see page 69)*.

### NO SENSE IN RUSHING

Balenciaga wasn't renowned for introducing something extreme and different every season, preferring to develop ideas over a period of time, tweaking and perfecting chosen silhouettes. However, for someone who was frequently labelled a formal classicist he was responsible for more than his fair share of fashion landmarks. In 1939 he was already working on the nipped-in waist, round-hipped jacket that would prefigure Dior's New Look. He was one of the first to put models in bodystockings (they've lived in them ever since). He also designed the classic sack dress, which must

### O ye of little Fath!

Another of fashion's classicists, Jacques Fath (1912–54) was famous for his plunging necklines, hour-glass silhouettes, nipped-in waists and full skirts. Like Balenciaga, he is credited with being a forerunner of the New Look. Givenchy (b. 1927) worked for Fath but is seen more as a successor to Balenciaga, with his simple, elegant outfits favoured by his muse, Audrey Hepburn. He is best known for his boat necklines and cropped sleeves.

Beaton shot this 1951 design.

Balenciaga's Air France outfit of 1966 was worn by over 1,300 air hostesses.

have been a welcome release for the corseted women of 1956.

While his daywear was wearable and often comfort-oriented, his evening-wear could border on the ludicrously impractical. Bustles, swags, balloons and puffs, heavy lace appliqué, feathers and flowers – wearers looked fabulous, but woe betide them if they tried to sit down in one of his creations.

**1905** The Cullinan diamond, the world's largest at 3,106 carats, is found near Pretoria, South Africa

**1914** The Raggedy Ann doll is created when American cartoonist John Gruelle draws features onto a rag doll's blank face and his wife Myrtle sews the words 'I love you' onto its appliquéd heart.

**1957** Hungarian actress Zsa-Zsa Gabor says 'I never hated a man enough to give him his diamonds back.'

## 1900~present

# Faking It

## More paste, less greed

*Costume jewellery has moved on from being a poor substitute for the real thing, to being a fashion accessory in its own right. Faking it has allowed designers and wearers a freedom of expression and a sense of humour that was previously limited by the constraints of cost.*

### Kenneth Lane

Despite having no technical experience (he originally worked on shoes for Dior and Roger Vivier), Kenneth Lane (b. 1932) became one of jewellery's most flamboyant and innovative designers. His oeuvre included earrings made from cotton wool covered with sequins, diamanté-encrusted animal brooches, gobstopper earrings, pearl rings the size of golf balls and enamelled shells. Nothing if not excessive, he adapted many of his designs from historical sources and brough. a strong feeling of theatricality to costume jewellery.

An over-the-top jewel-encrusted flamingo by Kenneth Lane.

**P**aul POIRET (1879–1944) was one of the first to experiment with costume jewellery, commissioning *Paul IRIBE* (1883–1935) to accessorize his clothes with distinctive tassel-style jewellery. The Poiret pendant, as it became known, was soon embellished with amber hearts, vegetable-dyed beads and stone buddhas.

Coco Chanel helped to make costume jewellery increasingly socially acceptable, by mixing and matching real and fake with insouciance. 'It does not matter if they are real, so long as they look like junk,' she said, as she

Earrings the size of a cranium. Fake jewels get too big for their boots.

incorporated Russian jewellery, crosses and rows of gilt chains in her outfits (must have been noisy when she ran for the bus!). Her arch-rival Schiaparelli was also keen on jewellery, working with her artist friends to produce a distinctive line of Surrealist pieces including telephone earrings by Salvador Dalí and lacquered eye shapes by Jean Cocteau. She used a huge variety of materials including feathers, lollipops, raffia cords, paperweights and rubber.

**1969** Zandra Rhodes launches her first collection, claiming to be 'tired of good taste'; motifs on her fabrics include lipsticks, teddy bears and hands.

**1980** There is a gold rush in the Amazon forest in Brazil and gold valued at 450 million is found.

**1996** Carol McFadden of Pennsylvania has collected 24,167 different pairs of earrings.

Irridescent paste accompanied Dior's New Look *(see pages 70–1)*, much of it designed by *Madame GRIPOIX*. Chandelier earrings, diamanté clips, massive bracelets and large ear clip-ons all became popular in the early 1950s. Humour was also important: jewellers Asprey introduced a washable bunch of plastic grapes in brooch form that was much worn in 1949.

By the early 1960s the trend was for throttling yourself with multiple strands of beads, which in turn gave way to Op Art jewellery. *Monty DON* played with *Liaisons dangereuses* style diamanté brooches and huge paste diamond drops finished with bows, while *Christian LACROIX* (b. 1951) produced extravagant baroque jewellery that became a symbol for 1980s designer

All that glitters is not gold (the diamonds aren't real either).

excess. The late 1990s has seen a return to more delicate styles with fine, filigree necklaces and vintage designer *Elsa PERRETTI* (b. 1940) is enjoying a renaissance with her delicate heart and drop motifs. Her designs have long been a staple of the most glamorous of all jewellers. Tiffany, in their more affordable ranges. *Paloma PICASSO* (b. 1949) has designed for Tiffany since 1980, creating styles using contemporary motifs sourced from graffiti and her famous kiss crosses.

## FASHION ESSENTIALS

In the mid 1960s jewellery was geometric, with black and white the favoured colours and perspex and dyed woods replacing traditional materials. This Op Art style was replaced by the eclectic nostalgia of Biba, Barbara Hulanicki's boutique, which revived 1930s style with flapper beads, plastic flower brooches and deco-inspired earrings.

When you're wearing this much exotic jewellery by Zanzara, why bother with the frock?

**1900** Latest dance craze is the cakewalk, which features couples doing high kicks as they parade down the dancehall.

**1912** Sarah Bernhardt stars as Queen Elizabeth I in her latest film; the movie makes an unprecedented profit of $80,000.

## 1898~1950
# Tinsel Taste
## Hooray for Hollywood

Back to the drawing board for cinema's most prolific designer Edith Head.

*During the so-called 'Golden Age of Cinema', Hollywood cast more of a well-groomed shadow on the world's dressing habits than any couture creation from the catwalks of Paris. Forget Chanel and Schiaparelli – it was the screen goddesses like Garbo, Dietrich, Crawford and Davis who sent women scurrying to the hairdresser, beauty parlour or sewing machine during the 1930s and 1940s.*

Puttin' on the glitz.

In the early days of movies, there were no costume designers and an actress with a serviceable wardrobe would get more roles than a competitor working out of a suitcase. Costume designers were only introduced out of necessity when popular stars, working fourteen hours a day, six days a week, weren't able to nip down to the local boutique for a spot of window shopping. As cinema-going increased so too did the fashion influence of its leading ladies, although all was not as it might seem from the other side of the

### Costumier to the Stars

During a career that spanned over fifty years and more than a thousand movies, costume designer Edith Head's credits rolled by on blockbusters such as *Vertigo, All About Eve, The Sting, Sunset Boulevard* and *Airport 77*. She began as a sketch artist for Paramount, later becoming the studio's leading designer before she moved to Universal. She dressed forty thousand extras in *The Man Who Would be King*, made a necklace for a snake in *The Lady Eve* and had her costumes eaten by hungry elephants

while working on blockbusters with director Cecil B. DeMille. Her designs sparked off a Spanish trend in the 1940s, and she got the world to adopt sarongs after Dorothy Lamour donned one for the 'On the Road to' series with Bob Hope and Bing Crosby. She won eight Oscars, and dressed almost every important star in Hollywood history, including Bette Davis, Liz Taylor, Mae West and Dietrich.

**1931** President Hoover thinks he has found a solution to America's economic troubles: 'What our country needs is a good big laugh.' His presidency ends in ruins.

**1944** French women who are accused of 'consorting with the enemy' during the German Occupation have their heads shaved.

**1949** Robert Mitchum is jailed for two months for smoking marijuana.

lens. Black and white film distorted colour so to achieve a true black on screen, the costumier would use carmine red – a shade which must have thrown a sinister light on all those celluloid funerals.

Talking pictures threw up their own slew of problems for the designer. Because of primitive sound recording techniques, fabrics had to be 'quiet' (no rustling taffeta allowed) and woe betide any bead or bangle that rattled during a take. Later still, Technicolor was criticized for making garments look too garish, and directors like Hitchcock would lose their tempers if a brightly coloured suit took away the spotlight from the actor. Despite the drawbacks, when Joan Crawford stepped onto screen sporting padded shoulders in the 1932 classic *Letty Lynton*, Macy's New York sold half a million copies of her dress within the year. When the actress enlarged her top lip with makeup to create 'the Crawford mouth', the look was widely copied (and still is by drag queens today). During the

### The Empire strikes back

Parisian fashion got its revenge on the studio system with the advent of Dior's New Look in 1947. Because most Hollywood films were made a year in advance, it wasn't until 1948 that audiences would see their movie idols wearing the wide skirts and nipped waists that were such high fashion.

same period countless women flocked to hairdressers for a Jean Harlow blond bob. Historical costumes tended to take on the look of the day: if a star playing Queen Elizabeth I fancied a perm and full 1940s makeup, or even a manicure and a low-cut evening-dress, she would get her own way. Movie idols started trends and as long as the Star System was promoted by studios, the audience emulated their heroes.

Jean Harlow wore a wig to hide a scalp badly burned by peroxide.

### STYLE ICON
⭐

*The skinny elfin little* **Audrey Hepburn** *(1929–93) started more than her fair share of fashion trends and popularized a look that is still imitated today: gamine haircut, capri pants worn with a black turtleneck sweater and flat pumps. She also invented the fashion for shirts worn knotted at the waist. On screen, she was memorably dressed by Edith Head in* Roman Holiday *(1953) and* Breakfast at Tiffany's *(1961) and the neckline she wore in* Sabrina *(1954), designed by Head, is still named after the film today.*

Audrey Hepburn kept her figure by eating ice cubes and lettuce.

**1928** British actress Hermione Baddeley causes scandal by wearing trousers at her wedding reception.

**1948** Daimler introduces electric car windows for the kiddies to shut their fingers in.

**1973** The wedding of Princess Anne and Captain Mark Phillips is the first royal wedding to be televised and is watched by 550 million people round the world.

# 1920~1998
# Royal Flush
## Monarchs of the glam

Norman Hartnell checks the drapes. Whoops, it's a dress, not a pair of curtains.

*The Windsors have always provided us common folk with a window on aristocratic style (although sometimes they might have been better advised to draw the curtains). The designers on whom they bestow royal favour revel in the reflected glory – for a while.*

### Our Norm

Appointed dressmaker to the British royal family in 1938, Norman Hartnell was primarily responsible for forming the style of both the Queen Mother and Queen Elizabeth II. He made not only the Queen's wedding dress and trousseau but also her coronation dress in 1953, which was lavishly embroidered with the emblems of Great Britain and the Commonwealth. Most at home with satin, tulle and embroidery, he also kitted out the royal family with conservative tweedy suits and coats. What a raver!

Edward (briefly) VIII's louche style and snappy suits caused a stir long before he married Wallis Simpson and became a sort of Dorian Gray style option to the worthy but stylistically dull George VI. Queen Elizabeth (the Queen Mum) never forgave Wallis for calling her the 'dowdy duchess' – a cruel reference to her life-time love affair with floaty lace and ruffles. Luckily for Elizabeth, *Norman HARTNELL* (1901–79) took her in hand and transformed her into the Winterhalter queen pastiching early Victorian dress, which suited her rounder figure.

The future Queen Elizabeth, with her handsome, slightly masculine face and figure, wasn't taking any chances, playing it safe in the fashion stakes with stalwarts *Hardy AMIES* (b. 1909) and Norman Hartnell. She was quite unlike 'bad girl' Princess Margaret who sneaked off to see Dior's New Look *(see pages 70–1)* in secret and wore a Dior ball gown for her 21st birthday. The Elizabeth Taylor of royalty, she was much copied in her youth until

Princess Margaret marries Antony Armstrong-Jones in a classic meringue dress.

**1982** Michael Fagan breaks into the Queen's bedroom in Buckingham Palace, steals a bottle of wine and asks her for a cigarette.

**1995** A Canadian chat show host poses as the prime minister and broadcasts his telephone conversation with the Queen in which he asks her views on Quebec's independence.

**1997** A dress belonging to Diana, Princess of Wales is sold for $200,000 by Christie's, New York, making it the most expensive frock ever.

a combination of middle-aged spread and Roddy Llewellyn led to an unfortunate flirtation with tropical islands and kaftans.

Prince Charles brought new meaning to the term 'old fogey', so it is surprising that he got married to (and divorced from) possibly the most stylistically influential woman of the 20th century – Princess Diana. A shy Di start was punctuated with too many silly tricorne hats, dodgy tights, ankle socks and a disastrous wedding dress (sorry chaps, but let's be honest) by *David* and *Elizabeth EMANUEL* (both b. 1953). This proved mere growing pains. By the time of her death she had progressed from the limited yet dutiful choices of a Princess promoting British fashion to a comfortable member of the jet set sporting everything from Versace, Ungaro, Lacroix and Chanel to old favourites Catherine Walker and Amanda Wakeley. Slavishly followed by the press, she reintroduced the fashion for tailored coatdresses and her chic signature blazer, tight fitted skirt and blouse became a popular look. It remains to be seen how

The woman whose face sold a million magazines at the centre of attention as usual.

## STYLE ICON

*The woman who coined the adage that you can never be too rich or too thin was, despite her lack of popularity, fêted as a style leader.* **Wallis Simpson** *(1896–1986) was drawn and photographed by Cecil*

Notoriously catty.

*Beaton and favoured severe, graphic little numbers by the top designers of the day. Her trousseau was by Molyneux and she also patronized Dior, Mainbocher and Schiaparelli who provided her the utterly simple suits she favoured. Wallis's favourite colour was blue and she had outrageously expensive tastes in jewels (don't we all?), which were supplied by Cartier and Van Cleef & Arpels, featuring everything from flamingos to big cat brooches. When her jewels were auctioned after her death it was one of the most publicized sales of the century. Calvin Klein bought her eternity ring and called a perfume after it (see page 33).*

her son William will fare in the fashion stakes (the press are keen to leap on faux pas), but what is certain is that in the style wars at least, Charles's chosen partner in joy, Camilla, is not in the competition.

**1901** Ransom E. Olds sells 425 Oldsmobiles, the first popular American car, for $650 apiece.

**1943** British *Vogue* advises readers to make the most of their clothing coupons by choosing a blouse and a skirt rather than a dress.

**1952** Edith Evans utters the immortal exclamation 'A handbag?!!!' in the film version of Oscar Wilde's *The Importance of Being Earnest*.

## 1900~present
# In the Bag
### Versatile status symbols

The Fendi croissant bag: after paying for it you can't eat for weeks.

*Whether it be Teletubby Tinky Winky, the Queen Mother or a fashion editor with the latest Gucci, the sociological significance of the handbag is at least as important as its function as an accessory. We have coined the term 'handbag house' to illustrate commercial dance music (girls who dance around their handbags in a nightclub are normally credited with dubious mental ability), and certainly in the UK, a man with a handbag will tend to have aspersions cast against his sexuality. Bolshie old ladies will clout you with them, transvestites dangle them from limp wrists and fashion victims enjoy the discreet but obvious charm of a tiny logo.*

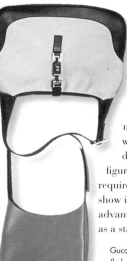

Of all accessories, the handbag is the most versatile and has the most tangible links to fashion. Unlike the most stylish clothing, which normally demands a svelte figure, a bag simply requires a shoulder to show it off to best advantage. And it doubles as a status symbol and a

Gucci (top) and Prada (below): iconic handbags of 1999. What's yours called?

disposable item that represents the look of the season. Every decade has its portable icon and as we enter the 21st century, the Italians have a tight clasp on the market.

Prada, Gucci *(see pages 128–9)* and Fendi *(see pages 114–15)* may all be perceived as fashion houses, but in reality

### Bags for men
In the UK or the US men and handbags don't mix – if you're not at least carrying the latest rucksack or combination lock briefcase, then you're hardly likely to accept a leather pochette dangling from the wrist as an emblem of masculinity. But, visit continental Europe and the men's handbag reigns supreme. At the local boule pitch or lying on the table at a pavement café, its black or tan leather design and simple shape is more likely to reveal a packet of cigarettes and a bunch of car keys than a lipstick and mascara.

**1979** Mrs Thatcher becomes Britain's first prime minister to carry a handbag – as far as we know.

**1985** Phil Collins releases a solo album entitled *No Jacket Required*.

**1990** A basket measuring 48 x 23 x 19 feet is made in Dresden, Ohio.

## STYLE ICON
★

*Grace Kelly (1929–82) started her career as a model, became a movie starlet and got to be Hitchcock's favourite icy cool blonde, before marrying a prince in 1956. That's the kind of lifestyle other women dream of emulating so it's no wonder that her (expensive) tastes in clothes were much copied. During the 1950s, the Hermès Kelly bag, named after her, was the epitome of high style, and even today when vintage examples come up for auction, the classic shape that has changed little over the past half decade will rival or exceed the price of the new.*

Bag lady *par excellence:* Grace Kelly loved her Hermès.

### FASHION ESSENTIALS

One of the joys of the handbag is the artisan quality it still retains for, unlike the multinational nature of so many designer brands, each fashion city has its own crop of designers making quirky, covetable and personal pieces that rival the companies that can afford to take out six pages of advertising in *Vogue*. When you're in Paris, check out Jamin Puech's 'inventive use of materials; in New York, Kate Spade for the holdall of choice for the young executive; and in London, Lulu Guinness's embroidered floral bags are favoured by our current crop of 'It girls'.

their clothing sales rarely make up more than 25 percent of overall income. It's the flashily logo-ed accessories and shoes that generate enormous sales across the globe – and if you're not convinced, pay a visit to Milan during the collections, when each store has been picked clean of merchandise by the fashion mavens who hover over empty shelves like vultures on the Serengeti.

For every costly purchase that has been carefully wrapped in tissue, emanating the rich fragrance of carefully tanned leather, there is a cheap copy, ostensibly the same, piled on pavements in markets as widely spread as Bangkok and New York (*see also pages 120–1*). But despite wholesale copying, the role of the accessory for the luxury house has underpinned the fortunes of some of fashion's contemporary figureheads.

1950s Hermès bag with 18-carat gold fittings.

The recent appointment of American designer *Marc Jacobs* (b. 1960) at Louis Vuitton has revamped a brand that once symbolized bourgeois good taste, and Tom Ford's reconstruction of Gucci, from tacky airport merchandise to a once-again desirable luxury brand, is one of the most-discussed legends of contemporary fashion.

**1939** Warner Brothers introduce cup sizing for brassieres.

**1940** Vera Lynn sings 'White Cliffs of Dover'. One comic jokes that 'the war was started by Vera Lynn's agent'.

**1942** The British are encouraged to 'Dig for Victory', planting vegetables in their back gardens.

1939~1945

# Land Girls
## The fashion ration

*Despite the threat of doodlebugs and the inconvenience of rationing, women still managed to indulge their fashion needs during the Second World War, often in extremely ingenious ways.*

Two women contemplate whether there's enough fur on the dog to make a nice little stole for winter.

The British government put a stranglehold on manufacturing and the words 'Utility' and 'rationing' hung heavily over the pages of fashion magazines. At first it was just silk stockings that went by the by, but in 1941 rationing was introduced with each adult allowed only 66 coupons annually. To put this into perspective, a woman's suit required 18 coupons. In June 1941, the depressing Utility clothing scheme was introduced, obliging manufacturers to make 85 per cent of their clothing in regulation styles and fabrics (hardwearing, i.e. not sexy).

## STYLE ICON
★

*Film star **Veronica Lake**'s long hairstyle characteristically dangling over one eye became the bane of the war effort. Women loved the style, despite its impracticality for work in factory and farm, and persistently continued to follow Veronica's example. A concerted campaign to picture film stars with hair obligingly rolled up and out of the way made little impact on fans. Some factories even introduced snoods to keep damage to a minimum and there were lurid tales of scalpings with Veronica-style hair getting caught in machinery.*

Peekaboo! It's the haircut Veronica's remembered for, rather than her films (like *I Married a Witch*, 1942).

**1941** Laurence Olivier and Vivien Leigh star in the patriotic *Lady Hamilton*. Winston Churchill says it's his favourite film.

**1942** US troops stationed in Britain are forbidden to drink the local milk because it is not pasteurized and they are worried it will cause diseases.

**1945** A plane flies into the Empire State Building, ripping a hole between the 78th and 79th floors.

Despite these privations there was a strong element of ingenuity and resourcefulness. 'Make do and mend' entered the vernacular as women set to patching, darning and refashioning anything they could lay their hands on. Woollens were unravelled and recycled, curtains were commandeered, coats were made from old blankets and shoes only survived with regular visits to the cobbler, or else had to be smuggled in from abroad.

### A bit flighty!

Silk and nylon parachutes became an essential source of fabric, deftly recycled as knickers, bras and night dresses. The long triangular pieces could be unpicked and restyled, although silk definitely had the edge over nylon. The black market was swamped with dodgy parachute material and another way of obtaining it was to work at the factories where they were made. By 1945 parachutes were on sale openly in shops along with instructions on how to get the most underwear out of the sections.

Finding cosmetics was a nightmare: some toiletries disappeared altogether and perfume was terribly scarce. The Government reduced the manufacture of cosmetics to a quarter of pre-war production. Hair was washed in soap and the black market boomed. Silk stockings became almost mythical. Women hated to be seen without them and many relied on American servicemen who, along with chewing gum and chocolate, seemed to have an inexhaustible supply. Some girls opted for leg makeup, painting their legs and drawing a seam down the back, while others used a paste of sand and water. Odd stockings were saved and re-dyed, and old stockings were refooted.

Most restrictions were only lifted in 1949. Demobbing in 1945 meant cash and clothing coupons for civilian life, but it took Dior's New Look *(see pages 70–1)* to break the hold of Utility – even if the majority of post-war women could only afford to look.

### GIRLS IN UNIFORM

Men were not the only people in uniforms, especially with the introduction of women's conscription for factory, farm and forces in 1941. Land Girls wore a distinctive kit of dungarees, canvas gaiters and green jersey (as well as a turban or two), a look that became synonymous with the war effort. For many women, it was their first experience of trousers (their own, at any rate). The armed forces, including the WRNS and the WAAF, wore uniforms with jackets similar to the men's, teamed with skirts and tunics.

Fieldworking land girls discover the joys of dungarees (plan ahead for comfort stops).

**1934** The world's first launderette opens in Texas with four electric washing machines.

**1942** The ballet *Rodeo* opens at New York's Metropolitan Opera House, with music by Aaron Copland.

**1956** Elvis the Pelvis makes his first movie, *Love Me Tender.* He gets shot in it, but reappears at the end as a ghost singing the title song.

1873~present

# Jean Genie

## A history of denim

Catering for gold diggers.

*For denim aficionados, the US patent number 139,121 given on 20 May 1873 has a certain resonance, as it signified the first official pair of Levi's. They were the brainchild of dry goods merchant Levi STRAUSS (?–1902) and Latvian tailor Jacob Davis, who first hit upon the idea of riveting pockets onto denim 'waist overalls' to prevent a difficult customer reportedly ripping the pockets from his trousers. Today jeans have huge sociological and emotional importance to customers worldwide.*

Denim, as we know it, purportedly owes its origins to the French 'serge de Nîmes', a serge fabric with a twill weave, originally woven from silk and wool, that was common in France at the end of the 17th century. It's believed the phrase was too difficult for English traders to pronounce when the fabric first arrived in England, hence the abbreviation to denim.

Even the term 'jeans' itself has a complicated and disputed etymology, possibly derived from 'Genoese', referring to the type of trousers worn by Italian sailors in the port of Genoa, or from the common name for denim fabric widely used to make workwear across the US in the 19th century. Certainly the word jeans has been used to describe any type of trouser made out of denim since the first

Nick Kaman, Levi's model and 80s pinup, giving it up for the girls. Ooh, those teeth.

**1967** At the height of the Vietnam War, sales of Ouija boards soar to 2.3 million.

**1983** Katherine Hamnett starts printing her ecological and political beliefs on T-shirts, such as the famous '58% don't want Pershing' one she wore to meet Mrs Thatcher.

**1997** Levi Strauss pay $25,000 dollars for some 501s that are believed to have been made between 1886 and 1902.

1950s teenagers looked like a Norman Rockwell painting.

### FASHION ESSENTIALS

Calvin Klein (see page 104) jumped on the jeans bandwagon in the 1970s, when Brooke Shields claimed 'Nothing comes between me and my Calvins'. Chanel showed denim suits and Versace launched a logo-ed brand; now you can buy Gucci jeans customized with Navaho embroidery and feathers, or custom-made Evisus, woven on vintage looms in Japan.

riveted pants were patented by Levi Strauss in 1873, but it was only in the mid 1950s when Levi's began advertising its products as 'right for school' that the term caught on across America (despite a widespread outcry from the conservative right). By the end of the 1950s, jeans had become part of the fabric of America, a 1958 newspaper claiming that: 'about 90 percent of American youths wear jeans everywhere except in bed and in church.' In Europe the cult was popularized during the Second World War by American servicemen wearing denims in their off-duty hours, and the widespread youth culture and rebellion engendered by the birth of rock and roll.

By the 1970s the trickle of jeans into Europe and Asia had become a flood. The traditional five pocket 'western' jean (a style which has changed little over the past hundred years) had evolved to encompass contemporary fashion and the bell bottom became de rigeur as traditional jeans brands began to incorporate non-denim products into their ranges. By the 1980s, the denim boom was out of control. Designer jeans were all the rage, offering the consumer the opportunity to buy into the mystique of a status symbol at a fraction of the cost. A slew of new fabric treatments produced surface effects such as 'acid wash' to complement the traditional ring-spun stonewashed styles. Today the term jeans can refer to anything, whether it be denim, printed satin or moleskin, and like any fashion phenomenon it has a following at all levels of the market, from the German manufacturer who incorporates an elastic waist for its larger ladies, to the vintage denim fanatics who have been known to fork out up to £10,000 for a particularly rare example.

Gucci jeans, 1999: ripped, frayed, tattered and embroidered.

**1943** Zoot suits provoke riots in Los Angeles and US servicemen attack anyone wearing them.

**1951** The Lacoste tennis shirt, imported from France, is an instant bestseller in the US.

**1968** Dick Fosbury wins the Olympic high jump for the US with his innovative 'Fosbury flop', leaping headfirst with his back just skimming the highjump bar.

1940~present

# Fast Fashion
## How to run a mile in style

Prototype bikinis: McCardell's loincloth beachwear of 1946.

*Two American designers achieved international recognition in the post-war scene – Claire MCCARDELL (1905–58) and Halston (aka Roy Halston FROWICK, 1932–90) – and sportswear became the hottest thing. The clothes were comfortable for lounging around in, even if you never broke a sweat, and useful for those who couldn't breathe in Dior's nipped-in waists.*

Claire McCardell rejected European style, opting for inspirations closer to home: pioneer calicoes, workmen's overalls and cowboy-style bandannas, plus clothes worn by sporting and comic book heroes (Dan Dare, Spiderman or Charlie Brown, the choice was yours). Although she designed resolutely for herself, she was fêted by American women who loved her comfortable, practical but stylish clothing. While working for the Manhattan-based manufacturer Townley, she came up with the bias-cut tent-like 'monastic dress', which sold out within 24 hours and became a design classic (ideal for those fuller figures after a Thanksgiving dinner).

McCardell excelled at working within wartime strictures *(see pages 60–1)*, experimenting with rugged hardware fasteners and surplus weather-balloon cotton. She was also ahead of her time in advocating easy-care, mass-production fabrics, the prototype of later American fashion design.

**1973** While playing for the Buffalo Bills, O.J. Simpson becomes the first football player to run more than 2,000 yards in a single season.

**1974** Muhammad Ali knocks out George Foreman in the eighth round of the so-called 'rumble in the jungle', thus regaining the world heavyweight championship.

**1988** Florence Griffith-Joyner, known for her ostentatious track suits and lethal fingernails, wins the 100 and 200m at the Seoul Olympics.

### FASHION ESSENTIALS

For the Claire McCardell look, adopt patch pockets, denim wraparound dresses, gingham shirts, high-waisted button-up slacks, jersey evening gowns, ballet shoes, empire line dresses, strap-less tube tops, fitted leather skirts, backless dresses and dirndl skirts. For Halston's look, think slinky jersey with halter necks slit to mid-waist, fitted cashmere sweaters in pale colours, kaftan and djebellah variations, tie-dyed chiffon halter-neck dresses, pant suits and shirtwaisters in Ultrasuede. Wear them all to go nightclubbing – or just sit back and relax.

McCardell girls wear ballgowns to frolic on the beach.

The greatest dancer: Halston's disco chic, 1975.

## SLINKY JERSEY

A very different designer, Halston started life as a milliner with clients including silent film goddess Gloria Swanson and Jackie Kennedy (he designed that pillbox hat). His first ready-to-wear collection was launched in 1966 and he soon developed the characteristic long narrow silhouette that would define American sportswear for the next decade. Halston became known as a designer of slinky knitwear, including turtlenecks and wide-legged jersey trousers, figure-hugging tunics, wrap-front dresses and his long, clinging, sheath halter-neck dresses. He was particularly fond of pliable fabrics such as wool jersey. By 1972, his reputation was legendary, not least for his regular attendance at cult club Studio 54. However, an unwise association with bargain department store JC Penney led to Bergdorf Goodman dropping his range and despite attempts to re-establish the golden years, Halston never succeeded in regaining his place in the strobe lights.

### Coming Klein

The designer who picked up Halston's mantle was Calvin Klein (b. 1942). Early on he specialized in coats and suits before breaking into the big time with his simple, softly tailored sportswear collections. The story goes that a buyer for Bonwitt Teller visited the wrong floor at the York Hotel, discovered Klein's workroom and immediately placed an order for $50,000. Klein quickly diversified and became king of the licence, as well as pioneering the craze for designer denim. His collections continue to keep to simple, carefully structured shapes in softly tonal colours without any fussy detail, and with a faintly androgynous feel that allowed him to move seamlessly into menswear in 1978.

**1946** The Flamingo Hotel opens in Las Vegas, funded by gang bosses Benjamin 'Buggsy' Siegel and Meyer Lansky.

**1950** A badly burned black bear cub is found in New Mexico and becomes 'Smokey the Bear', a symbol for advertising campaigns to prevent forest fires.

**1954** Clouds of radioactive dust fall on the Japanese fishing boat *Lucky Tiger* after US hydrogen bomb tests in the Bikini Atoll.

**1955** Synchronized swimming becomes a competitive event at the Pan American Games in Mexico City.

1946~Present

# Itsy Bitsy Teeny Weeny

## Let's have a thong thing

Radioactive fallout.

*Who'd have thought that a series of nuclear tests carried out on a tiny atoll called Bikini in the South Pacific would become associated with one of the most evocative pieces of clothing of all time? Bikinis had, of course, been brewing for quite a while, with styles cropping up on Roman wall paintings and later designs for beach suits preceding the idea, but it was a mechanical engineer called Louis Reard who actually had the smarts to patent his design in 1946 and have it modelled by a stripper.*

The bikini's made of Bri-Nylon and the model's made of plastic.

I t was launched simultaneously by *Jacques HEIM* (1899–1967), who called his version the 'atome', proving that both men thought they'd hit on explosive stuff.

**GOSSIP** While sunlovers everywhere instantly embraced the bikini, the Catholic church condemned the new style. Actress Esther Williams said she wouldn't be seen dead in one (bit out of place in a funeral parlour), and post war Britain wasn't going to risk a furore so the first Miss World Contest was held with everyone in chaste one-pieces. But it didn't take long for a favourite bikini pastime to be established when Robert Mitchum removed a starlet's bikini top at Cannes in 1954. Eight years later the itsy bitsy polka dot bikini was immortalized in an otherwise forgettable pop song.

Reard's first attempt was outrageous for the time and not far away from the string bikinis of the 1970s. He subsequently opened a shop in Paris, which sold over 100 different styles.

The bikini became the perfect vehicle for starlets to show off their goods: Marilyn Monroe, Rita Hayworth, Diana Dors (who had a mink one made for her) and Jayne Mansfield all wriggled into the tiny scraps of fabric with glee.

Styles have always flirted with the ridiculous. Bikinis became the best way to make the newspapers in the summer months, with women wearing propeller-

**1961** Nappy-laundering services are driven out of business after the launch of disposable Pampers.

**1977** It is estimated that 10,000 'boat people' are fleeing Vietnam every month in dangerous, leaky ships.

Whatever tickles your fancy: a design by Freud.

bladed bikini tops, stick-on handprints, butterflies and pussycats in strategic places. Union Jacks, edible bikinis, hedgehog skins and real hair bikinis. As a reality check, the shop-bought styles of the day were a lot more controlled. In the 1950s, they looked like a Laura Ashley interior, all frills and floral chintz with pointed structured bras and detailing just about everywhere.

In the 1960s there was a craze for crochet, as well as the low-belted hipster style, but fabric was being severely eroded with more and more flesh on show until the advent of the terrifying G-string and thong. Strapless bikinis were popular, reducing strap lines before the serious advent of topless bathing.

*Liza BRUCE* (b. 1955) made sophisticated swimwear from Lycra, crêpe and silk, while *Norma KAMALI* (b. 1945) brought

us the infamous wet-look bikini. The 1980s were dominated by the introduction of Day-Glo and new crinkle fabrics that stretched to fit when worn.

Lycra transformed the bikini, making the fit far better; metallics were introduced and retro looks (influenced by 1920s and 1930s styling) were experimented with. Bikini bottoms were rolled down to just above the pubic bone and Brazilian beaches became famous as the home of the mini thong. Despite the increasing acceptance of topless bathing, it seems the bikini is here to stay.

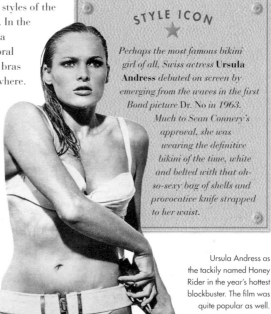

## STYLE ICON
★

*Perhaps the most famous bikini girl of all, Swiss actress* **Ursula Andress** *debuted on screen by emerging from the waves in the first Bond picture Dr. No in 1963. Much to Sean Connery's approval, she was wearing the definitive bikini of the time, white and belted with that oh-so-sexy bag of shells and provocative knife strapped to her waist.*

Ursula Andress as the tackily named Honey Rider in the year's hottest blockbuster. The film was quite popular as well.

**1944** *Seventeen* magazine caters for teenagers who want to read about 'dates and shyness, rather than atomic energy'.

**1949** The first edible vegetable protein is made from soybeans.

**1953** Raymond Chandler writes in *The Long Goodbye*: 'Alcohol is like love: the first kiss is magic, the second is intimate, the third is routine. After that you just take the girl's clothes off.'

1940s~1970s

# A Touch of Pizzazz
## Diana Vreeland

*During a long career at* Harper's Bazaar, *American* Vogue *and latterly as curator of costume exhibitions at the Metropolitan Museum of Art in New York, Diana VREELAND (1906–89) evolved as a role model for every aspiring fashion maven. Novelist Truman Capote described her as 'the kind of genius that very few people will ever recognize because you need genius yourself to recognize it. Otherwise you'll think that she's rather a foolish woman.' She epitomized the glamour and superficiality that is commonly associated with the world of fashion reportage and, if her personality was a little larger than life, so too were her achievements.*

## The glossies

The first issue of *Vogue* appeared in the US in 1892 as a weekly fashion magazine for women of society. British *Vogue* followed in 1910 and the French, Australian, Spanish and German editions were hot on its heels (although the Spanish and German editions folded after a few issues). *Vogue* went on to become the 20th century's most influential fashion bible, closely followed by *Harper's Bazaar*, which was founded in 1867. *Women's Wear Daily*, originally a trade magazine, was sold to the public from 1960. Reliant on advertising, the glossies were rarely politically controversial, preferring to reflect the status quo, as in the pre-First World War editions that criticize the antics of the suffragettes and assert that a woman's place is in the home.

Vreeland first achieved notoriety in the mid 1930s, with her frivolous column for *Harper's Bazaar* entitled 'Why don't you...' that was full of wacky suggestions and bon mots designed to cheer and amuse a society still emerging from a bleak period of economic recession (see box for examples).

In 1939 she was appointed fashion editor on the magazine, a post she retained for 23 years, before becoming Editor-in-Chief at American *Vogue* in 1963, where she immediately began to stamp her idiosyncratic personality on the visual and editorial content of the magazine. If you wanted wild stallions with blue mono-fibre manes, then so be it. Vreeland's edict was all in

Putting the bizarre in *Bazaar*: la Grande Dame in 1933.

**1960** Antonio Lopez brings the bold style and humour of Pop Art to fashion illustration.

**1969** In Wisconsin, the average dairy cow produces 10 quarts of milk a day; in 1940 it was only 6.

**1975** Jimmy Hoffa, who created the Teamsters Union of American truckers, disappears one night; it is believed that he is murdered by gangsters.

favour of experimentation when it came to matters visual. She had a keen eye for talented photographers, designers and models. In particular she invented the notion of beautiful people (or BNPs as they came to be known) and coined phrases such as 'pink is the navy blue of India', which have since been immortalized by fashion historians. Her moods were

legendary: she once sacked an assistant for wearing squeaky shoes, and her reign at American *Vogue* was regarded with as much terror as it was admiration. Sadly this all came to an end in 1971, when publishers Condé Nast decided that a new generation of career women needed an editor with a less aspirational and more realistic view of fashion. They said 'Why don't you ...' and Vreeland was ignominiously dismissed only to reappear later that year as special consultant to the Costume Institute of the Metropolitan Museum of Art, where she staged a series of exhibitions that attracted a multitude of visitors.

Vreeland showing Balenciaga's one-seam coat, MOMA, 1973.

At their most successful, such as the 1979 Ballets Russes show, these were responsible for altering fashions on the catwalks. A striking woman, with a beak-like nose and a smear of crimson lipstick, Vreeland remained the doyen of American high fashion, receiving numerous honours and awards. She published a book about fashion, *Allure* (1980), and *DV* (1984), her autobiography, which has been criticized as a 'name-dropping lie' but is amusing reading nonetheless.

## FASHION ESSENTIALS

Some of the best Vreeland bon mots:

☞ Why don't you have your cigarettes stamped with a personal insignia as a well-known explorer did with his penguin? (July 1936)

☞ Why don't you paint a map of the world on all four walls of your boys' nursery so that they won't grow up with a provincial point-of-view? (July 1936)

☞ Why don't you rinse your blond child's hair in dead champagne to keep its gold as they do in France? (July 1936)

☞ Why don't you give the wife of your favourite band leader a jazz band made of tiny baguette diamonds and cabochon emeralds? (December 1936)

☞ Why don't you go out in the snow with a court jester's hood of cherry red cotton velvet? (January 1937)

☞ Why don't you wear violet velvet mittens with everything? (February 1937)

☞ Why don't you in your drawing room have a mirror table like [the actress] Miss Constance Collier's, with a diamond pencil so that your guests can sign their names in the glass? (April 1938)

Great ideas, Diana. Why not indeed?

**1947** Margaret Mitchell, author of *Gone with the Wind*, is killed by a drunk driver while crossing the street in her home town Atlanta.

**1948** The first Jewish state since biblical times, Israel is created from territory that was previously part of Palestine.

**1950** Bathing and shaving are banned in New York in an attempt to ease the city's water shortage.

## 1947~1958
# New Look
### The French Revolution

*Although fashion has always had the power to provoke, only one designer has been responsible for a style that was denounced by British politicians and caused widespread social unrest, protesters dismissing it as wasteful and constrictive. The New Look was a stroke of genius by Christian DIOR (1905–57). After the deprivations of the war, nothing could have been more shocking than the acres of fabric needed to make his wide skirts or tiny, nipped-in jackets. New Look dresses needed 10, 25, even as many as 80 yards! 'Never mind the war,' adverts could have run, 'feel the width.'*

The hottest name in Paris. Dior's New Look collection was dubbed 'the Battle of the Marne of couture'.

**B**orn in Normandy to a wealthy family, Dior's first contact with the world of couture came in 1934, when he shared an apartment with designer Jean Ozenne. Fascinated by fashion, he began to play around with sketches, selling them to, among other people, the couturier

Robert Piguet, who immediately employed Dior as a designer. The Second World War interrupted his progress when he was drafted into the French army. After the war he secured a job with *Lucien LELONG*

Accessories were important, from the lampshade worn on the head to bunion-creating stilettos.

### Bar to Barbie
The single design that most embodied the New Look was called 'Bar'. It was a suit consisting of a natural silk pongee jacket with unpadded shoulders and a corseted waist that created an hour-glass figure, promoted by padding round the hips in a peplum style. The jacket was worn with a wide, pleated skirt that rested at mid-ankle length and teamed with black gloves and pointed stiletto shoes. Other designers had played with this eveningwear look, but Dior hit it lucky with his post-war timing. When Barbie dolls were introduced in 1959, this was one of the first looks fans could dress them in.

**1952** The Rolodex is invented; this revolving cylinder changes the face of office filing.

**1955** A car spins out of control during the Le Mans 24-hour race and kills 85 spectators plus the driver.

**1958** Englishman Cyril Northcote Parkinson coins Parkinson's Law: 'Work expands so as to fill the time available for its completion.'

(1889–1958) but soon found the backing to strike out on his own. He leased 30 Avenue Montaigne and the House (or should I say Kingdom) of Dior was born.

Success was immediate, generated from a single collection, which proclaimed Dior's ethos on fashion, much inspired by his childhood and the fashions of his youth. The New Look was initially called the 'corolle line' because it was based on an upturned flower. The theme was continued in Dior's evening dresses, which were flights of fancy with long bouffant skirts and impossible layers of tulle, while day dresses had wide skirts and neatly nipped-in waisted jackets. It was perfect timing. Women were sick of the war and longed to indulge themselves. The New Look fitted the bill perfectly for those with ample dosh.

## FASHION ESSENTIALS

Dior became well known for his carefully planned themes featuring new innovations. For 1947 he pulled waists in ever-tighter while in 1948 he experimented with asymmetry, turning up collars and working with shorter lengths. In 1949 he used separate panels to give the illusion of a fuller skirt without the actual bulk and worked on wide lapels and collars. Other key Dior looks include knife pleats, horseshoe collars, belts on the back of coats and jackets, boxy suits and pleated skirts. For evening and daywear he favoured faux empire lines, the princesse line, open tulip skirts and scooped necklines. The H line, with its long moulded body, was dubbed the Second Look and he also advocated A-line chemises in 1957.

Women made a beeline for the A-line.

Dior's last wish was to be replaced by the young *Yves Saint-Laurent* (b. 1936), who many now regard as the last great couturier. This ensured that the House of Dior would continue to be associated with innovative design, and the reign was continued with the appointment in 1996 of British designer *John Galliano* (b. 1960).

Galliano gets all theatrical in his 1997 collection for Dior.

**1953** There are at least 100,000 stores in the US where pizza can be bought.

**1957** Alberto Moravia publishes *Two Women*, a story about Italian refugees at the end of World War II.

**1959** Fellini's film *La Dolce Vita* includes some memorable scenes: Anita Ekberg in the Trevi Fountain with a kitten on her head; Nadia Gray doing a striptease at an orgy; and a statue of Christ flying over Rome.

1800s~present

# Let Your Hair Down

## Poodles, perms, mods and Mohicans

*The L'Oreal catchphrase for its haircare products 'Because I'm worth it' is a telling comment on how women perceive their hairstyles, for a trip to the hairdresser can represent an affordable form of psychotherapy and is widely believed to raise the spirits, whether it's a wash and set with a blue rinse for a trip to the local whist drive or a foot-high concoction for a West End film opening.*

The most-discussed hair of the late 1990s: 'Friend'ly Jennifer Aniston's streaked and layered bob.

Vidal Sassoon shows off his handiwork, 1975.

Since the 19th century, a woman's hair has carried more social importance than that of her spouse. The 'man as peacock' ethic of the 18th century had given way to the Industrial Revolution, the powdered wigs of yore were boxed up, fleas and all, and while the newly short-haired husbands went out to work, the ponderous and complex hairstyles of the spouse who stayed at home to supervise the servants became a form of social status.

When the shorter bobbed styles of the 1920s emerged, the first women to adopt the look were reviled by the church in tracts that stated it was both against God and nature (quite right too). As women's emancipation increased in tandem with the growing access to media, hairstyles became increasingly fashion led.

During the 1950s and 1960s hair was crazily coiffured. London was the birthplace of the celebrity hairdresser in the guise of *Vidal SASSOON* (b. 1929), who popularized the three-point bob, and the more esoterically titled Mr Teasy-Weasy, who was the society hairdresser of his day. Hairstyles adopted names like dances. There was the poodle (no prizes for guessing what it resembled), the elegant

**1962** Sophia Loren and Carlo Ponti are charged with bigamy, following their 1957 marriage.

**1968** Germany produces 2.5 million cars; Japan 2.1 million; France 1.8 million; Britain 1.7 million; and Italy 1.5 million.

**1969** Mario Puzo writes about the Mafia in *The Godfather* – and lives to tell the tale.

French pleat and the beehive. Hippiedom brought beads, bunches and lank fringes in the late 1960s and early 1970s, only to be challenged by the onslaught of Punk *(see pages 108–9)* at the end of the decade. Suddenly ugly was cool, sugar and water turned tresses into sticks of spiked rock candy, and the bravest opted for superglue for the sharpest spikes on the highest Mohican. Although a few Punks remain today, primarily for the benefit of American tourists who will happily pay a couple of quid for a glimpse of the 'sordid underbelly' of London, by the 1980s hair had pumped up the volume with the help of back-combing and hairspray. Suddenly the 'Dallas' and 'Dynasty' aesthetic *(see pages 122–3)* made cinema and theatre audiences groan when the focus of attention was obscured by a frizz of permed hair in the front row. At the salon, rubber showercaps with watering-can piercing popularized highlights and enormous plastic pincer combs pulled bunches of unruly permed hair into perilously high hair-don'ts.

By the 1990s, fashion's confusion with its future made it turn to re-examine its origins,

and the ensuing historical pastiches of antiquated hairstyles enabled wannabe Edwardians, Rockabillies and Mods to reinvent these styles. Youth culture decreed 'anything goes'.

The starfish look: a spectacular mohawk photographed in California, 1992.

## STYLE ICON
⭐

*In the 1960s, the hairstyle icon was* **Dusty Springfield**, *with her perfect beehive worn with lashings of heavy black mascara and frosted pink lipstick. In the 1970s Farrah Fawcett Majors's shaggy, layered look had schoolgirls heating their Carmen rollers nightly. The punk icon was, of course, Jordan (see page 109), although Boy George (see page 119) started his own trend for dreadlocks.*

'Charlie's Angels': hairstyles that relied on heated curlers and ozone-damaging sprays.

**1960** Following her husband's inauguration, Jackie Kennedy says, 'The one thing I do not want to be called is First Lady. It sounds like a saddle horse.'

**1963** Nightclub owner Jack Ruby shoots Lee Harvey Oswald before he can be tried for the murder of JFK.

**1969** Baby-food manufacturers in the US stop using monosodium glutamate after tests show that it causes brain damage in mice.

1950s~1980s

# Shopping and Shipping
## Jackie O

Fateful events in Dallas, 1963.

*Jacqueline Lee Bouvier Kennedy ONASSIS (1929–94) is a fashion icon of our time: an elegant debutante in satin gloves and a string of pearls; a tragic high priestess of style in a blood-splattered suit; a shipping magnate's wife in oversized sunglasses and headscarf. For many of her devotees she has become a symbol of the American aristocracy: patrician in bearing, an accomplished horsewoman, 'debutante of the year' for the 1947-48 season – and stinking rich to boot!*

After graduating from Washington University, she took a job as 'inquiring photographer' for a local newspaper; she soon encountered senator *John F. KENNEDY* (1917–63) and married the future president in a furore of publicity in 1953. From then on, Jackie O and her peculiarly American style were subject to the closest scrutiny. As the new First Lady, she wisely chose New York-based designer *Oleg CASSINI* (b. 1913) in preference to the Paris couturiers she secretly favoured, and thence a style that defined a decade was born. Reports of her extravagance were widespread but she rebutted some, claiming she couldn't possibly spend $30,000 dollars a year on fashion 'unless I wore sable underwear'.

Jackie with her son John-John, who died in a flying accident in 1999.

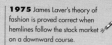

**1975** James Laver's theory of fashion is proved correct when hemlines follow the stock market on a downward course.

**1975** New York City is brought to a standstill by a power blackout that lasts 25 hours.

**1984** Andrew Lloyd Webber's *Starlight Express* opens in London with performers on roller skates pretending to be trains.

Today those massive 'bug' specs are affectionately known as 'Jackie O's'.

Think of Jackie O and the image is of a slightly built woman with a figure sculpted from years of horseriding, a simple dress silhouette often sleeveless or with a wide scoop neck, a string of pearls and a pillbox hat perched on a bouffant hairdo. Her oversized sunglasses and headscarves were so popular during her lifetime that even Marguerite Oswald, mother of Lee Harvey, adopted the combination when she embarked on incognito research junkets to exculpate her son, wearing what she called with unintended irony 'her Jackie Kennedy disguise'. After she retired from public life during her marriage to Greek shipping magnate *Aristotle ONASSIS* (1906–75), she was rarely seen in public without large black-framed sunglasses. Although the boxy suit she wore during the fateful assassination of her husband is probably the best-remembered outfit of her career,

the simple pieces – such as Cassini's fawn wool two-piece outfit, a dress and waist-length semi-fitted jacket or coat with a removable round-neck collar of Russian sable, often topped by the infamous braided pillbox hats created by Halston *(see page 65)* – were the styles that put American fashion on the map in the 1960s.

### FASHION ESSENTIALS

During the spring of 1996, Sotheby's New York auctioned off 5,914 items belonging to the estate of Jacqueline Lee Bouvier Kennedy Onassis, in a sale which attracted 40,000 Jackie O fanatics to pay homage from the public viewing galleries and generated over $34.5 million dollars (the pre-sale estimate had been $4 million). One of the most famous items was the faux pearl necklace immortalized in a photograph of John F Kennedy Jr toying with it around his smiling mother's neck. Linda and Stewart Resnick, owners of the Franklin Mint Museum based in Philadelphia, bid $211,500 for a piece that had only been expected to fetch between $700 and $900, claiming it reminded them of the innocence of the 1960s. For those of you who hanker after the style, but not the financial outlay, they are now producing reproductions of the same necklace for $195 a time.

After her marriage to Onassis in 1968, Jackie re-located to New York where she lived quietly until her death, working as an editor for the publishers Doubleday. The fame that had once illuminated her life now became a burden of responsibility: 'I don't want to be a fashion symbol, I just want to be appropriately dressed,' she said. 'Clothes are a nuisance to me.'

**1956** Cliff Richard's 'Living Doll' is the UK's top hit of the year.

**1957** Graham Greene's play *The Potting Shed* opens in New York, starring Sybil Thorndike.

**1958** The Notting Hill Riots take place in London in August and September.

1955~1965

# Mods & Rockers

## Britain's wild ones

*The strongest youth culture looks in Britain couldn't have been more opposite: Mods liked neat, Italian-style suits, parkas and motor scooter while Rockers liked leather and chair You wouldn't have thought it was something to fight about, but it all ended in tears with fighting in several British seaside resorts in 1964; at a subsequent trial the judge called them all 'little sawdust Caesars'.*

Brando's cult 1953 movie helped to inspire the Rockers' look.

**Make my day, punk!**
The antipathy between Mods and Rockers was forever immortalized by cult film *Quadrophenia* (1979), starring Sting and Leslie Ash. It captured the battle between the two factions and was instrumental in promoting a revival of two of youth culture's strongest 1960s looks. Many style observers see the uncompromising attitude of the Rockers as a direct predecessor of Punk *(see pages 108-9).*

Mods looked to the future, to jazz and cult European style, not least the signature Italian suits and the favoured mode of transport, the Lambretta scooter. Styles for men and women blurred, with the emphasis on slick, modern looks and sharp minimalism, including short Roman jackets, no-turn-up trousers with

Fists of fashion: Mods gather on Brighton beach, 1965.

**1961** The old black and white five-pound notes are withdrawn from circulation in Britain and replaced with blue ones.

**1962** An Essex schoolboy dances the Twist for 33 hours non-stop.

**1964** Harold Wilson becomes prime minister; he is seldom seen without a pipe in his mouth.

17-inch bottoms, pointed shoes or boots and crisp stone or white macs. Women wore sporty short hemlines, little blazer jackets and hair cropped short to the face, influenced by film stars like Jean Seberg, while makeup was pale and interesting. Mod style has been revived on a regular basis ever since, not least in the early 1980s with Paul Weller's take on their sharp monochrome looks, although the Mod label was becoming increasingly linked to people wearing moccasin shoes and parkas with Who insignia sewn on.

'n' roll icons like Elvis. Black leather biker jackets were a trademark, customized with studs and aggressive painted insignia such as skull-and-crossbones or knives. Outrageously pointed winkle pickers, blue jeans with turn-ups and chains all became synonymous with the Rocker look. While the Rockers may have been hopelessly outnumbered by Mods in the summer of 1964, their style can still be seen in many a garage forecourt and biker pub.

## STYLE ICON
★

*The archetypal Rocker icon,* **Marlon Brando**'s *drawling uncommunicative biker in* The Wild One *was seen as such a threat to society that despite being made as early as 1953, the film was effectively banned in Britain until 1968. The classic line when Brando is asked what he is rebelling against and he replies 'Whaddya got?' is backed up by the Brando Rocker look – a leather jacket complete with his embroidered name, tight trousers, biker boots and peaked cap (and an obligatory scowl).*

The definitive motorcycle rebel with his name on his jacket, in case he forgets it.

The rival looks of the Rockers were kept hard and confrontational, mixing bike culture with rock 'n' roll by the likes of Billy Fury, Gene Vincent and Eddie Cochran, rejecting what they saw as the watered-down sell-out by supposed rock

**1959** Gunter Grass's novel *The Tin Drum* tells of a strange child who stopped growing at the age of three, constantly bangs a tin drum and has a scream that shatters glass.

**1965** Joseph Beuys presents his performance piece *How to Explain Pictures to a Dead Hare* in which he walks through a gallery carrying a dead hare and explaining the pictures to it.

**1969** The phrase 'ego trip' is first used to denote an action that is self-centred or self-obsessed.

1955~present

# Karl Lagerfeld
### Germany's fashion chameleon

*Behind the aloof, almost caricatured façade and trademark fan, Karl LAGERFELD (b. 1938) is a designer of extreme discipline and versatility, who has had a considerable influence on haute couture – partly because he's worked for most of the couture houses in his time.*

Fan the Man. Hiding his light behind the infamous accoutrements or basking in the glow of success?

Lagerfeld gives his model the cold shoulder in a stark evening wear design for Chloé.

### FASHION ESSENTIALS

Rococo shepherdess dresses; scarves tied round the bust, waist or shoulders; luxurious kimono-style reversible fur and leather coats; reclaimed mini skirts; layered skirts over trousers; bright colours, especially red! Lagerfeld takes classic styles and adds his own quirky touches.

Restless migrations from one design house to another have been a characteristic of Lagerfeld's career. In 1954, he won the top prize for a coat design sponsored by the International Wool Secretariat. Designer Pierre Balmain *(see page 31)* picked up the young Lagerfeld, put his coat into production and hired him as a design assistant. After three years, Lagerfeld moved to Patou *(see page 32)* as art director. This, too, did not last long and, bored by the world of haute couture, he left for Italy to study art.

He was lured back by Chloé, a house that was looking to fuse haute couture with the ever-growing market for prêt-à-porter. He also worked as a freelance designer for Krizia, Valentino and shoe designer Charles Jourdan, before joining Fendi as a consultant designer in 1967. But it was in 1983 when he became design director for Chanel that he really came into his own, breathing new life into the ailing and stale collections.

**1976** Ulrike Meinhof of the infamous Baader-Meinhof gang hangs herself in prison; at her funeral, thousands of sympathizers paint their faces white or wear masks.

**1983** The magazine *Stern* announces the 'Hitler Diaries' to be fakes after the *Sunday Times* has paid £1 million for serialization rights.

**1998** Claudia Schiffer sheds her clothes to advertise a car; it is later revealed that she had a body double for her feet and an actress dubbed her voice.

He designed both the couture and ready-to-wear lines and his collections were generally regarded as a tour de force. It was only in 1984 that he launched his own label, preferring previously to impose his mercurial nature on other people's houses.

Lagerfeld made his mark on Paris couture by taking the essence of an established house and twisting it on its head, creating a very personal interpretation but one that still has the cachet and recognition of the long-established label. That is not to say he is not capable of innovation – he was an early exponent of underwear as outerwear, playing with silks, see-through layers, camisoles and slip dresses. Bright colours are a big deal with Lagerfeld, witness his sugar pink and acid green take on Chanel suits, along with a dramatic use of red in his own collections. He's partial to Schiaparelli-style embroideries, such as diamanté guitars, running taps and hammers, and his playful takes on the revered Chanel logo have seen the classic Cs appear on wellington boots and tiny bikinis. Will he stick with Chanel? Or will the wanderlust strike again?

The Chanel suit given the Lagerfeld treatment. What would Coco have to say?

Lagerfeld posing with a gaggle of supermodels at a Chloé show in 1994.

## GOSSIP

Lagerfeld was destined for a life in the surreal world of couture. Practically from birth, he astonished his businessman father by behaving like a little Lord of the Manor. One childhood story relates that he decided that he wanted a valet as his fourth birthday present. When this was denied, he began to instruct a fantasy valet in the art of ironing his shirt collar. It is hard to tell how much is true affectation with Lagerfeld and how much is real; his obsession for silk fans has reached epic proportions (he is rarely seen without one) and he's one of those celebs who sports his dark glasses indoors and out.

**1955** Marilyn Monroe cools down over a subway vent and poster designers never forget it.

**1966** Michael Caine's career as a Cockney womanizer is launched with the movie Alfie; he is the first star to wear glasses since Harold Lloyd.

**1973** Brigitte Bardot retires from film to devote herself to animal welfare. She says 'I leave before being left. I decide.'

1950s~present

# The Celluloid Catwalk

## Celebrity style

Liz Taylor
as Cleopatra.

*It's often claimed that the sequels are pale imitations of the originals but in the case of cinematic fashion, the cast may change but the influence on our wardrobes remains the same. By the mid 1950s the enormous influence of Hollywood studio designers on fashion was waning, as costume luminaries such as Edith Head (see pages 54-5) were asked to reinterpret historical pastiches rather than generate new ideas of their own. Fashion was once again led by the ateliers of Paris rather than Los Angeles, and instead of celebrating home-grown talent, film moguls began to draft in designers from abroad to add necessary aplomb to their masterpieces.*

Edith Head sketches another exotic
sarong for Dorothy Lamour.

Yves Saint Laurent's work on Luis Buñuel's 1967 *Belle de Jour* made actress Catherine Deneuve *(see page 91)* an instant fashion icon. Audrey Hepburn enjoyed a long working relationship with designer *Hubert de GIVENCHY* (b. 1927), most famously in *Breakfast at Tiffany's* (1961). Robert Redford was dressed by Ralph Lauren *(see page 104)* in *The Great Gatsby* (1974), Madonna by Dolce & Gabbana *(see page 128)* for *Evita* (1997) and Helen Mirren indulged in a little light S&M courtesy of Jean Paul Gaultier *(see page 95)* in Peter Greenaway's *The Cook, The Thief, His Wife and Her Lover* (1989). But whether designers' links with studios actually influence grass-roots fashion is still open to debate.

**1981** Duran Duran release the single 'Girls on Film' and Simon LeBon becomes pin-up of the year.

**1992** Sharon Stone famously uncrosses and recrosses her legs in Basic Instinct.

**1996** For the film *Evita*, Madonna wears 45 pairs of shoes, 56 pairs of earrings, 39 hats and 42 different hairstyles. She changes her outfit 85 times.

Kate Winslet sparks a jewellery trend and Leo DiCaprio enflames teenage girls.

The easiest trends to trace are the historical reworkings that have the power to transform the inhabitants of a local shopping precinct into characters from a Jane Austen novel but some films influence dress in more subtle ways. Nobody today would be willing to adopt the Edwardian ensembles worn by Kate Winslet in the weep-fest *Titanic* (1997), but the delicate jewellery and teardrop earrings were an instant commercial hit. Similarly when Meryl Streep played the ill-fated Karen Blixen in *Out of Africa* (1985), fashion suddenly got a taste of the dark continent's hinterland, safari gear and all.

As we enter the new millennium, cinema and fashion remain in close association. After all, fashion is a major focus for the media, so it's no surprise that it has relevance at the box office. We have movies on the fashion system itself, such as Robert Altman's *Prêt à Porter* (1994), supermodels stepping from editorials to cinematic cameo roles, such

as Shalom Harlow playing herself (creditably) in Kevin Kline's comedy *In and Out* (1997), and even designers allowing the lens to follow the run-up to a show, such as Isaac Mizrahi's cinematic debut in *Unzipped* (1995). And then of course there's character merchandising – but does a Teenage Mutant Ninja Turtles tracksuit qualify as fashion ?

Catherine Zeta-Jones wows them in Versace at the 1999 Oscars.

### The Oscars
There is fierce competition among designers to dress the leading ladies in a show-stopping number for the Oscars. Subject to as much speculation and reportage as the Academy Awards themselves, the right gown on the right celebrity will pay more dividends than any number of pages of advertising in the glossies. Some actresses remain faithful to a particular designer, such as Jodie Foster's long-term association with Armani, while Sharon Stone confounded the critics one year by opting to wear a T-shirt from The Gap. Some are applauded for their choices and others are villified. As for Cher, who's usually dressed in a deeply revealing beaded creation designed by Bob Mackie (b. 1940), the critics are divided between applauding her sense of the dramatic and looking for the latest evidence of plastic surgery.

**1960** The number of dressmakers in the US is one-third of what it was in 1900 and the number of working women has doubled.

**1968** California furniture designer Charles Prior Hall investigates the qualities of vinyl and liquid starch and within two years he has perfected the water bed.

**1973** For the first time, more vodka than whisky is sold in the US.

## 1958~present
# Fabrics With Attitude
### New age material

*Late 20th-century fabrics often defy belief, coming across as a curious mixture of Buck Rogers meets Star Trek. A million miles from the cheap and cheerful world of drip dry, this is high tech at its most techy – smart fibres with minds of their own.*

If you need protection, you can bet someone will have developed a fabric to suit you. Scared of the awesome power of UV rays? Some fabrics have a built-in UV protection factor of 30+ and in Japan (the spiritual home of techy fabrics) they've

Skin-tight lycra catsuit and criss-cross go-go boots. Wonder what her clothes are thinking?

Techy top by Miu Miu, the younger face of Prada.

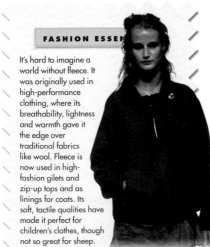

**FASHION ESSEN**

It's hard to imagine a world without fleece. It was originally used in high-performance clothing, where its breathability, lightness and warmth gave it the edge over traditional fabrics like wool. Fleece is now used in high-fashion gilets and zip-up tops and as linings for coats. Its soft, tactile qualities have made it perfect for children's clothes, though not so great for sheep.

adapted a treated polyester organza originally developed for the car industry that protects you from skin cancer. Even more space age is micro-encapsulation fabric, originally developed for use in space travel, which contains capsules that can be absorbed into the skin. Choose from useful vitamin C, smart seaweed extracts, and now even a fragrance encapsulation that releases scent and should last for around thirty washes – so make sure you like it.

**1976** Bjorn Borg, known as the 'Iceborg' for his cool temperament on court, wins his first Wimbledon title at the age of twenty.

**1983** Christo circles eleven islands in Biscayne Bay, Florida, with bright pink fabric and calls them 'my water lilies'.

**1996** Primitive worm casts found in a meteorite suggest that Earth may have been invaded by Martians around 13,000 years ago.

## Socks save the universe!

With the Western world's anxiety about evil micro-organisms waiting to pounce at any moment and the media obsession with superbugs and viruses, it's not surprising that fabrics are being developed to deal with our late-20th-century paranoia. New textiles – such as Amicor Plus, developed by Courtaulds Fibres – have active anti-bacterial and anti-fungal properties. Blended with cotton, these are already used for the manufacture of socks and underwear. Many of the new fibres can control unwanted odours and appear in boot liners and high performance underwear. Science at its most considerate.

If you tend to get too hot or too cold, there's a new technology being developed to enhance the thermal efficiency of fleece, jackets, socks and outerwear. These new fabrics programme a kind of microclimate creating a thermal barrier around the body and maintaining a comfortable temperature while preventing overheating. Ceramic particles are also being used to regulate temperature and new levels of breathability and waterproofing are being introduced all the time. Sweat, too, has been targeted. 'Moisture management', as it is rather coyly known, works by drawing sweat away from the skin and dispersing it to evaporate as soon as possible. Heavier fabrics such as canvas are getting the anti-sweat treatment and some nylons now feature a finish that permanently bonds water molecules and quickly disperses them.

Fun fur. Certainly more fun for minks, foxes, sables and squirrels.

While many fabrics started life as sports or outward-bound high-performance clothing, the benefits of these hard-working garments appeal to a wider market and have become a keen selling point for fashion clothing. The future seems wide open to developments. New ideas include anti-stress calm-inducing fabrics, vitamin- and beneficial-oil-impregnated clothing and even clothing that acts as a mini health visitor, checking up on the physical state of the wearer. Science fiction? Probably not, but we're still waiting for the day when our clothes can decide what we should wear in the morning and choose their own co-ordinating accessories – or even decide they're too good for the likes of us.

Cheesy family wear new age fabrics in cult TV series *Lost in Space*.

**1959** William Burroughs's *The Naked Lunch* is a surrealistic portrait of drug addiction.

**1962** The first hovercraft carries passengers across the Dee estuary from Rhyl to Wallasey.

**1965** Englishman Craven Walter exhibits his Astrolight, in which gobs of molten coloured wax rise and fall in an illuminated cylinder. As the Lava Lite, it will feature widely in Sixties interiors.

1959~1970

# Quantum Leap
## Why the chicks love Mary

*For many people, Mary Quant was the 1960s. Although she had hardly any practical dress-making experience, she hit exactly the right note with her cheap, fun clothes aimed at a previously ignored market – the teenager. Especially the skinny teenager.*

The Queen of Swinging London in 1965.

Fashion-obsessed from an early age, Quant allegedly chopped up a family heirloom bedspread with nail scissors because she thought it would look better as a dress. After college, she toyed with millinery before deciding to open her legendary first shop, Bazaar, on London's King's Road in 1955 (with her future husband Alexander Plunket Green). She initially sold fashions by other designers, but found that they didn't fit in with what

STYLE ICON

City gents buy shares in kohl as the panda look rules supreme.

*Little **Leslie Hornby** (b. 1949) was the Kate Moss of her time, the archetypal wide-eyed waif beauty. Weighing in at just six and a half stone, it wasn't hard to see where she got her 'Twiggy' nickname, and her bony, childlike body was perfect for the new mood of the 1960s. She became one of the first models to popularize Quant's new mini skirts, worn with her geometric haircut from Vidal Sassoon (see page 72). Pre-empting the supermodels of the 1990s, she appeared on the cover of Time magazine, was dubbed the face of 1966, had her own range of makeup, clothing and hosiery, had a doll named after her – and all this before she retired from modelling at the ripe old age of 19, so she could have a square meal for a change.*

**1966** Raquel Welch fends off dinosaurs wearing a fetching suede bikini in *One Million Years BC*.

**1968** The Beatles' 'Hey Jude' is UK hit of the year, supposedly written for John Lennon's son Julian.

**1970** Man-made fibres account for 56% of US fabric production, up from 28% in 1960. Polyester is the most popular, at 41%, with cotton production at only 35%.

she perceived as the new look for the youth market, so she decided to produce her own.

The business was run in a brilliantly fly-by-the-seat-of-your-pants style. Dresses were made up at night, brought in to Bazaar first thing in the morning, often sold out by 6pm, and the money was then used to buy fabric from Harrods to make up the next day's stock. Quant was reputedly so terrified of her customers in the beginning that she used to keep a bottle of Scotch under the counter. Once the ice was broken, customers joined in and the atmosphere at Bazaar became more cocktail bar than boutique.

Quant wasn't scared of breaking down the old social mores. She discarded the gilt-backed chairs and salon atmosphere that had always dominated fashion shows and sent models parading down the catwalk to cool jazz instead of tinkling classics. Her clothes too were perfect for the time. She loved very simple, very bright shapes with plenty of geometric designs,

### FASHION ESSENTIALS

Mary Quant never claimed to have invented the mini – she always gave credit to the girls who embodied swinging 1960s London. Its development has been attributed to André Courrèges (b. 1923) and John Bates (b. 1938), but it was Mary Quant who brought it to the attention of the world. Starting just above the knee in fairly modest fashion, it crept up the thigh between 1965 and 1970 and was considered positively shocking by the establishment. It was embraced by youth culture as its quintessential uniform until competition from the maxi made it seem like old hat.

made the mini skirt into a mass trend and started a fashion for kooky coloured tights, skinny rib sweaters, crochet tops and hipster belts. She was ahead of her time with fabrics, experimenting with PVC for little macs and separates.

Quant made it big in the US where she designed lines for JC Penney and in later years was perhaps best known for her brightly coloured cheaply priced cosmetics, all featuring her daisy logo. She continues to design today, principally for the Japanese market, but posterity will always herald her as the woman who invented teenage fashion.

Which one is the belt? And what if you drop your bus ticket? The mini quandary.

**1961** Rudolf Nureyev escapes from his Russian minders in Le Bourget airport, Paris, and throws himself into the arms of two French policemen asking for asylum.

**1967** Jacques Derrida's books *Speech and Phenomena, Of Grammatology* and *Writing and Difference* introduce the principle of deconstruction.

**1974** TV series Kojak introduces the lollypop-sucking, bald detective who calls people 'pussycat' and asks 'Who loves ya, baby?'

1960~1990

# Haughty Couture
### Unaffordable fashion

The front row of a couture show can be more interesting than the clothes.

*Haute couture is a loss-leader for the fashion industry. Few designers expect that the exquisite made-to-measure pieces shown on the catwalks in Paris and Rome will turn in a profit, but the publicity that they generate is ample repayment for the losses incurred. Those who spend up to £30,000 on a frock include the sheikh's wife who will wear an item just once in the privacy of a purdah tea-party; the New York social X-ray hosting a cocktail party in her Upper East Side apartment; and the former film star and friend of the designer, who buys garments at a sizeable discount and wears them out of a sense of loyalty.*

Prior to the advent of ready-to-wear in the 1950s, haute couture represented the pinnacle of fashion, when names such as Dior *(see pages 70–1)* and Pierre Balmain *(see page 30)* determined the silhouette of the wealthiest women. In 1946 there were 106 couture houses but by 1997 there were only 18. Today designers consider themselves lucky to sell a handful of dresses each season from a couture collection, although a new generation of

younger couturiers are combining the made-to-measure aspects of the craft (numerous fittings, linen or muslin toiles, hand-applied decoration) with less bohemian and more wearable creations. If you extend the definition of couture to cover anyone creating made-to-measure garments, the market becomes wider: a wedding dress is couture even if it has been hand-sewn and fitted in a bedroom in Pontefract rather than a Parisian atelier.

**1981** France's TGV train starts running to Lyons at speeds of 236 miles per hour.

**1986** Greg LeMond becomes the first American to win the Tour de France cycle race.

**1990** Coco Chanel's last words are 'You see, this is how you die.'

### What the designers say . . .

☞ 'Haute couture is finished because it's in the hands of men who don't like women.' Coco Chanel, 1967

☞ 'A designer who is not also a couturier, who hasn't learned the most refined mysteries of physically creating his models, is like a sculptor who gives his drawings to another man, an artisan, to accomplish.' Yves Saint Laurent, 1984

☞ 'Haute couture should be fun, foolish and almost unwearable.' Christian Lacroix, 1987

Not many of us are willing to purchase a frock that costs the equivalent of a small semi-detached house when the high street soon copies the best looks. Yet even if haute couture is unapproachable for all but the privileged few, it still garners headlines and column inches because it is such a valuable breeding ground for new ideas. It represents the ultimate in fantasy for designers – fashion for fashion's sake alone – and allows them the indulgence of creating one-off showpieces. A couture dress may carry 500,000 seed pearls each hand-beaded by traditional companies such as Lesage (see box). Fabric suppliers will donate metres of their most extraordinary materials for publicity purposes, and it's not unusual to see macaw feathers garnishing a neckline at Gaultier

(*see page 95)* or rods of fine Venetian glass at Versace (*see pages 126–7)*. And even if the latest Chanel suit or Lacroix ballgown serves as the female status symbol equivalent of a wealthy husband's red Ferrari, they are more than purely idle decoration. For while old ready-to-wear has little value once it's paid a couple of visits to the dry cleaners, vintage couture has become a highly collectable investment, often equalling its cost price at auction.

Fashion with a flourish: Lacroix is the industry's supreme decorative artist.

### STYLE ICON
★

*When Schiaparelli wanted astral symbols in gold and silver lamé embroidered on her coats or when Yves Saint Laurent wanted Picasso faces on evening dresses, they turned to the Parisian firm of **Lesage**. Founded in 1868 and still thriving in the 1990s, the embroidery house has worked with all the great couturiers, from Worth and Vionnet through to Lacroix. The price is not cheap, but if your eveningwear needs a glitzy Midas touch without looking like a Dame Edna Everage number, these are the people to turn to.*

**1960** The new city of Brasilia, designed by Oscar Niemeyer, becomes capital of Brazil.

**1961** Henry Mancini writes the song 'Moon River' for the film *Breakfast at Tiffany's*.

**1963** Anthony De Angelis of the Allied Crude Vegetable Oil & Refining Company is found guilty of fraud for using seawater instead of oil in his salad dressings.

## 1960s
# Spaced Out
### Courrèges, Rabanne and Cardin

*The high modernism of Pierre CARDIN (b. 1922), André COURRÈGES (b. 1923) and Paco RABANNE (b. 1934) seems touchingly innocent when viewed through the jaded perspective of the end of the century. Science and technology in contemporary culture signify something far removed from the faith and hope in the future that Rabanne experienced with his self-conscious use of Space Age materials. Likewise, Courrèges and his minuscule shifts scattered with Pop Art daisy motifs and Cardin's hard-edged constructivist garments imbue us with a nostalgia for the optimism in new technology embraced in 1960s design.*

Pierre Cardin

Today, Paco Rabanne may be better known for his numerous and successful ranges of toiletries, but his innovative use of plastic and metal forged a new area of expertise and has influenced the work of a number of contemporary designers including

A simple little futurist number by Courrèges, 1964. Note the fab boots.

Alexander McQUEEN (b. 1969) and Martine SITBON (b. 1951). Rabanne prefers to be called an engineer rather than a designer, and his garments are more like Space Age prototypes than wearable clothes. It is estimated that by 1966 he was getting through 30,000 metres of Rhodoid plastic per month in his wild designs such as bib necklaces made of phosphorescent plastic discs strung together with fine wire and whole dresses of the same material linked by metal chains.

The legacy of Courrèges is inevitably linked with the invention of the mini skirt (*see pages 84–5*), but his understanding of the contemporary woman's wardrobe has

**1965** The International Society for Krishna Consciousness is started by A. C. Bhaktivedanta, who sits on a pavement chanting 'Hare Krishna' and instructs his followers to shave their heads and wear saffron-coloured dhotis.

**1967** The wreck of the *Torrey Canyon* off Cornwall is the world's biggest oil spillage, with oil reaching as far as the coast of France.

**1969** Octavio Guillén and Adriana Martinez get married in Mexico City after a 67-year engagement. They are both aged 82.

as much to do with Chanel's earlier appropriation of menswear classics for a female audience *(see pages 42–3)*. Following a philosophy of freeing rather than containing, he created revealing, childlike clothes for the emancipation of play girls and the visual stimulation of play boys, that may resemble Barbie outfits today but were a radical simplification of style for their time.

Pierre Cardin's impact has been eclipsed by a long and ludicrous line of licensed products *(see page 121)* but his design work epitomizes the curiously asexual modernism of the mid 1960s. He had a sculptural approach to cut and construction (arguably echoed in the work of Japanese designer Issey Miyake, *see page 106*). His interest in man-made fibres culminated in the creation of his own fabric in 1968, a bonded uncrushable fibre incorporating raised geometric patterns, modestly entitled Cardine. More importantly, his Nehru jackets for men were adopted by the Beatles and fast became de rigeur for the fashionable 1960s man, complete with turtleneck and sideburns.

Ultimately, the vision that made these designers the

Paco Rabanne

**FASHION ESSENTIALS**

Rabanne's version of chainmail using tiny triangles of aluminium and leather held together with flexible wire rings to construct a series of simple shift mini dresses remains popular today, except at airport baggage scans. The Courrèges style was ultra-simple: shift dresses, tunics with trousers, patch pockets, big yokes, chevron stitching, strange baby bonnets and flat white patent leather boots. Cardin's 1964 Space Age collection featured tabards over leggings, knitted white catsuits and tubular knitted dresses.

Rabanne used pliers rather than a needle and thread to work with his wacky fabrics.

vanguard of modernism during the 1960s now looks the stuff of TV re-runs, as dress has become more cynical and less childlike in ensuing decades. However, without their experiments, the pendulum of fashion might have slowed our progress, and instead of taking a pragmatic approach to the fashions of the future, we could be stuck in perspex bonnets, aluminium dresses and strange itchy synthetics – no fun on the 8:20 rush hour train to Charing Cross.

**1960** Jean-Luc Godard's *A Bout de Souffle* uses new cinematic techniques to tell the old story of a car thief who goes on the run with his girlfriend.

**1963** Wigs become fashionable. *Vogue* claims 'A little fakery these days means a whole lot of chic.'

**1967** Black or white wet-look leggings are worn with patent or wet-look shoes, instead of boots.

1960s~present

# All About Yves

### The reclusive genius

A bespectacled Christ figure: Yves Saint Laurent in 1969.

*Were a Hollywood studio considering making a designer biopic, the complex tale of Yves Saint LAURENT (b. 1936) would be ideal fodder. And yet, if his story resembles a morality tale of how the life of a designer is like that of a butterfly strapped to a wheel, one must not forget that YSL's contribution to fashion in the latter half of the 20th century has been colossal. In redefining the way in which women dress, he has, like his predecessor Chanel, appropriated ideas from the masculine wardrobe, transforming them into wearable, chic classics such as 'Le Smoking', a feminized adaptation of the tuxedo; safari jackets; brass-buttoned pea coats; and a fantasy take on ethnicity, which sanitized tribal culture for a Western audience.*

### Naked chic

Back in 1971 Yves Saint Laurent shocked audiences by appearing nude in adverts to launch his new men's fragrance 'YSL'. Shot by photographer and friend Jeanloup Sieff, the advert features a black and white portrait of YSL sitting on a leather cushion, and was shot with such graphic intensity that even the veins in his hand were picked out. Originally Saint Laurent wanted to position the bottle between his legs, but according to Sieff: 'I explained why I thought that wouldn't work.' Nevertheless some magazines refused to run the advert, claiming it was unsuitable for children, while others called the designer a cherub, or a bespectacled Christ. Despite this, the adverts succeeded in underscoring YSL's reputation as a daring and glamorous role-model for the young.

At the tender age of 19 he became a design assistant at Dior, and two years later was thrust into the full media spotlight when Christian Dior died, and Saint Laurent suddenly became the creative force behind Paris's most revered couture house. After his first collection of 1958, entitled 'Trapeze', he was popularly heralded as the saviour of couture, but the second 'Arc' line was less well received and the 'beat look', unveiled in 1960, outraged conservative Dior clients and heralded YSL's prompt departure to the French army. After less than three weeks in barracks, he suffered a nervous breakdown

**1972** Tiny blonde athlete Olga Korbut elicits sighs of sympathy around the world when she falls from the parallel bars during the Munich Olympics, but she goes on to win gold on the beam and in the floor exercises.

**1983** David Boyce travels from central Paris to central London in 38 minutes, 53 seconds, travelling by motorcycle, helicopter and Hawker Hunter jet.

**1996** A bomb explodes on the Paris Métro, killing two and injuring fifty. It is believed to have been planted by Algerian Islamic fundamentalists.

and spent the following month-and-a-half tranquillized and bedridden in a high security mental hospital. Better fortune followed in 1961: he won a legal suit for unfair dismissal against Dior and, in conjunction with partner Pierre Bergé, founded the Yves Saint Laurent empire.

During the 1960s YSL went from strength to strength, launching the ready-to-wear line Rive Gauche in 1966. 'Y' became the first of a long list of fragrances. Over the ensuing decade, as his commercial success escalated, so did his reclusive nature and dependence on artificial stimulants and tranquillizers; as Bergé described it, he often suffered 'overwhelming nervous exhaustion'. In the late 1990s, Saint Laurent experienced a renaissance: he handed over the creation of Rive Gauche to Israeli-American designer Alber Elbaz and his fragile health seems to have stabilized. If contemporary Saint Laurent is more about re-interpreting the classics that have made his an interstellar career, his continued contribution remains enormously influential and he acts as a godfather (in the nicest sense of the word) for new designers worldwide. His mantra of colour, cut and class have endeared him to millions, his fragrances are a bathroom fixture and his life a mixture of tragedy and hedonism that adds to the overall mystique of one of fashion's most reclusive and fascinating designers.

## STYLE ICON
★

*In the 1960s, YSL began a life-long friendship with French actress **Catherine Deneuve** (b.1943), who wore his clothes in the celebrated film Belle de Jour (1967) and became his muse and vendeuse mondaine (i.e. she promoted his designs by wearing them to the 'right' parties). Other famous partnerships of this type include Wallis Simpson and Mainbocher (see page 57); Princess Caroline of Monaco and Dior; Elizabeth Taylor and Valentino; and Liz Hurley and Versace (see page 126).*

Deneuve plays a bored housewife turned prostitute.

Getting boa-ed in YSL's 1971 black smoking suit.

**1964** The first edition of 'Top of the Pops' is broadcast. Dusty Springfield, the Rolling Stones, the Hollies and the Dave Clark Five appear.

**1965** Designer Rudi Gernreich claims 'Bras have been like something you wear on your head on New Year's Eve.'

**1969** The first 'hot pants' appear, worn under a split midi; they are given their name by *Women's Wear Daily* in 1971.

1960~1985

# Disco Dollies
## Strut your Spandex

*Although it's roots are embedded in 1960s dance culture, disco fever first took off as an underground movement in 1973. By the time the world saw John Travolta kitted out in white suit and snazzy black shirt in the film* Saturday Night Fever *in 1977, disco fever had gone well and truly global.*

It's a tragedy. I bet they still ask John Travolta to do this at parties.

### Get your rah-rahs

Norma Kamali (b. 1945) opened her first boutique in 1967 and soon became established as designer to the stars with her theatrical, eye-catching designs. Her clothing was perfect for the disco era with styles like gold lamé maillots, her penchant for leopard skin and her cultish parachute-nylon jumpsuits worn open at the neck. She also reinvented the mini skirt for a new generation with the introduction of the cheerleader-inspired rah-rah. Kamali was a pioneer of the broad-shouldered proportions that were to become popular in the early 1980s and favoured jersey for its strength (it wouldn't split in Travolta poses).

Disco had become more than just a club label: there was now dedicated dance music and multimedia dance experiences with strobe lights, mirror balls and dry ice. This very theatrical style of clubbing was bound to engender a demand for clothing that could stand out and show off the increasing body aesthetic that had developed alongside the dance music *(see pages 102–3)*. Top disco looks blurred sexual boundaries and indulged in new levels of posing and

| **1971** Vivienne Westwood and Malcolm McLaren open a shop called Let It Rock in London's King's Road; the following year they rename it Too Fast to Live, Too Young to Die.  | **1973** Pina Bausch founds the dance company Tanztheater Wuppertal; they use experimental body language and expressionistic moves. | **1985** Polystyrene coffee cups, aerosol propellants and fridges are all blamed for the hole in the ozone layer.  |

Stephen BURROWS (b. 1943) is associated with disco style, with his leisure clothing and bright separates designed to show off the body, while Betsey JOHNSON (b. 1942) moved out of the swinging 1960s straight into disco wear, which provided the perfect showcase for her loud colours in stretch jersey.

Bo Derek with beady hair in the film *10* (1979).

Roller disco: responsible for more broken ankles than platform trainers?

theatrical-inspired costumes. Although it is often dismissed as the decade that style forgot, 1970s disco-wear has continued to be influential on fashion and it was perhaps the first key American look that developed a strong following in Europe.

The most memorable disco looks included moulded all-in-one body leotards, wrap-around skirts tied at the waist, T-shirts cut short and worn over bodies and the shortest, hottest hot pants. Spandex provided the necessary strength along with Lurex, rayon and Lycra, while the lights begged for sequins, diamanté, rhinestones, garish prints, body glitter spray, wet look lip gloss and bright dayglo colours. Hair was braided and beaded or streaked with multi-colour spray (which made it clump together in sticky locks).

## DISCO DESIGNERS
Although disco fans chiefly created their own looks, mixed and matched from dance gear, several designers caught the mood.

### STYLE ICON
★

**Studio 54** *was the disco nightclub of the 1970s, opened in an abandoned New York theatre in 1977 and run by the flamboyant Steve Rubell. Designed for people who wanted to be seen, the disco floor had a voyeuristic balcony around it and a VIP lounge where you could meet celebrities such as Calvin Klein, Andy Warhol, Bianca Jagger (and Mick) and Liza Minnelli. Though it lasted for less than two years, Studio 54 was the blueprint for thousands of replicas that cropped up across America and Europe.*

**1966** The Kray twins shoot George Cornell in the Blind Beggar pub, in London's East End.

**1970** The British army fire rubber bullets for the first time during disturbances in Belfast.

**1977** Rita Hayworth is made a ward of her daughter Yasmin while she receives treatment for alcoholism.

1960s~present

# Kinky Gerlinky
## Fetish leaps out of the closet

*Fetish clothing used to consist of little bits of rubber and leather that were bought covertly, worn at special clubs or in the privacy of the home and brushed under the carpet by the rest of society. However at the beginning of the 1990s there was a quantum shift in the way people thought about fetish. Suddenly leather and rubber came out of the closet and designers from Helmut LANG (b. 1956) to Thierry MUGLER (b. 1948) started experimenting with some of the wilder derivations of S&M.*

Thierry Mugler meets *Metropolis*: his designs are renowned for accentuating the female body.

Originally the clothes worn in bondage and S&M clubs like London's famous Skin Two were elaborate coded messages about the type of fetish the wearer was into. Dominatrices carried leads for their slaves, the corset was inverted as a symbol of feminine power and high, impossibly stilettoed shoes were heaven for foot fetishists. Visually stunning pornographic images floated on the edge of counter culture and it was only a matter of time before first photographers and then designers picked up on them.

*Vivienne WESTWOOD* (b. 1941) got the bit between her teeth (almost literally) when her Punk collections adapted fetish items such as peep-hole trousers

### FASHION ESSENTIALS

Leather's S&M image began in the mid 1960s when the delectable Honor Blackman gave off dikey vibes in a tight black leather number in *Goldfinger* (1964). Diana Rigg caused a stir in her outrageous plastic and leather creations in the cult TV series 'The Avengers'. And the pop world caught on to leather's shock value when Marianne Faithfull appeared clad in very little else in the film *Girl on a Motorcycle* (1968).

Quintessential rock 'n' roll chick Marianne Faithfull zips up her leathers.

**1982** Grace Kelly, Princess of Monaco, dies when her car spins out of control on a hairpin bend in the principality.

**1990** The catchphrase 'Damn fine cup of coffee' becomes popular, from the weird American TV series 'Twin Peaks'.

**1998** Rock star Michael Hutchence is found hanged in a Sydney hotel room.

and PVC tops. Pam Hogg took up Westwood's combination of Punk and S&M and ran with it into the 1980s, producing several fetish-inspired collections. Helmut Lang *(see pages 116–17)* combined fabrics and blurred the distinctions between men's and women's clothing. The highly structured leather, wide shoulders and selective padding of the work of *Claude MONTANA* (b. 1949) and Thierry Mugler provided the logical bridge into mainstream for fetish clothing, emphasizing the waist and pulling in corsetry.

Enfant terrible *Jean Paul GAULTIER* (b. 1952) had a ball with sex club clothing and the bridge from sub culture to mainstream was complete with the wholesale adoption of several crucial corsetry styles by the high-street shops. By 1995 fetish-inspired looks were available on the mass market, prompted by cheaper and more comfortable innovations in rubber, latex and plastic (you no longer had to coat yourself in talcum powder to wriggle into them). PVC cat suits and dresses, stilettos and lace-up boots, bustiers and leather hot pants or trousers,

> ## STYLE ICON
> ⭐
>
> *Always on the look-out for a way to reinvent herself, pop's Material Girl went further than anyone to regularize and sanitize fetish clothing. With plenty of help from Jean-Paul Gaultier,* **Madonna**'s *1990 Blond Ambition tour was a paean to fetish with pointed conical bras in flesh pink and gold. Madonna played the dominatrix on stage, whipping her dancers into a frenzy, her pinstripe suit slashed to show black bondage bra underneath. Rather than leave it there, she felt the need to play out her S&M fantasies in her much-discussed (and oft-ridiculed) book,* Sex.

Madonna's image changes are often more memorable than her music.

lace-up corsets, rubber bras and cut-out, peephole dresses were turning up on the catwalks of everyone from *Paco RABANNE* (b. 1934) to *Azzedine ALAÏA* (b. 1940). Today even nice girls can't resist the appeal of rubber trousers.

**2000 BC** The first
nose reconstruction
plastic surgery is
performed in India.

**1955** American singer
Diamanda Galàs is born. She will
have a tattoo on her knuckles that
reads 'We are all HIV positive.'

**1990** Johnny Depp is
reported to have a tattoo that
reads Winona in honour of his
then girlfriend Winona Ryder.

## 2000BC~present
# Piercing Looks
## Tattoos and body modification

Orlan plans her next
operation; cut along
the dotted lines.

*Throughout history humans
have decorated themselves with
tattoos and body modifications
but it was only towards the end
of the 20th century that these
became high fashion, from the
minuscule butterfly that flutters on
the ankle of a supermodel to full-
scale facial restructuring courtesy
of French performance artist
Orlan, who has undergone
at least nine bouts of
plastic surgery, including
modifications to make her face resemble
that of the Mona Lisa and Venus (can't
see it, can you?).*

A ttitudes have changed towards body
modification. Today a tattoo signifies
a new form of tribalism, which has little in
common with the traditional motifs used
by sailors or servicemen, but is an
acknowledgement of ethnic cultures
worldwide, made popular by the rise of
foreign tourism and the 1960s hippie
propensity for adopting a more permanent
form of decoration than love beads.
A tattoo is a permanent symbol of self,
whether it be a discreet Celtic cross on
the upper arm or a fourteen-colour
extravaganza etched with the patience and

### Serious suffering
Beyond traditional piercings
and tattoos, new methods of
body modification that are
growing in popularity
include scarification, in
which cuts applied to the
skin are prevented from
healing properly leaving a
raised Braille-like decorative
scar; and branding, where
hot metal is literally burnt
into the skin (one tattooists'
textbook recommends
practising on a chicken
breast before trying the
technique on human skin,
and responsibly suggests
that if you're vegetarian,
tofu will do). Please form an
orderly queue.

The ideal
decoration for
the girl who
wants to make
her mark, but
discreetly.

**1991** A 5,000-year-old corpse found in the Austrian Alps has tattoos on its back, knees and ankles.

**1994** Marge Schott, owner of the Cincinatti Reds baseball team explains why she doesn't let her players pierce their ears: 'Only fruits wear earrings.'

detail of an Old Master. It can symbolize a form of fraternity, as in the tattoos worn by members of the Japanese Yakuza (or Mafia), or it can be purely decorative, etched in henna or *mehndi* and guaranteed to fade after a fortnight. Ironically, many of the traditional ethnic tattoo designs are more prevalent now in Western tattoo parlours than in their native cultures. While we yearn to become modern primitives, developing cultures are increasingly rejecting their ancient forms of body modification.

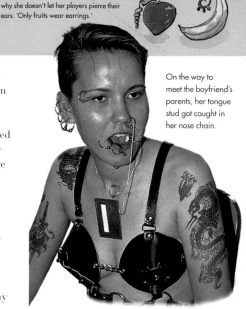

On the way to meet the boyfriend's parents, her tongue stud got caught in her nose chain.

Piercings are also a growth industry. Their long history takes in the Roman centurions who wore nipple rings as a way of keeping their cloaks in place and the widespread practice of *apadrayra* (a piercing of the penis) which features in the *Kama Sutra*. Pierced ears have long been commonplace, even on toddlers, but pierced belly buttons, eyebrows and noses have only become popular since Punk icons the Sex Pistols sported safety pins *(see page 108)* and Girl Power, courtesy of the Spice Girls *(see page 41)*, had seven year-olds begging their mothers for pierced tongues. More intimately, items like the guiche and the Prince Albert (see box) may not be significant enough to set off the metal detectors at the airport but are nonetheless a popular choice because of the heightened sexual enjoyment they purportedly give the wearer.

Finally, of course, there's the home-made tattoo, for which all you need is a pair of compasses, a bottle of Indian ink

and a low IQ. And if you're now regretting an emblem on your skin made in haste while a teenager, tattoo removal is available using laser surgery. But do remember that, like a diamond, a tattoo is normally forever; what cost you £50 on a drunken revel, is likely to cost over £1,000 to have removed.

### FASHION ESSENTIALS

The Prince Albert piercing is a ring inserted through the urethra that moves or rotates. In the Victorian era it was used to strap the penis tightly to the leg to minimize the bulge when wearing tight trousers. Rumour has it that Prince Albert wore one to hold back his foreskin and keep his member smelling sweetly so as not to offend Her Majesty Victoria.

**1964** Animal lovers protest after President Johnson lifts his two pet beagles by the ears during a White House press conference.

**1964** Roy Lichtenstein produces the comic-strip painting *Good Morning, Darling*. He is inspired by mass-produced items like bubblegum wrappers.

**1965** *Cosmopolitan* magazine is launched, urging readers to 'Have fun, be single and have sex'.

1964~1967

# Factory Floor
## Trash Fash

*Not since the 1920s has an artist had more impact on the fashion scene than Andy WARHOL (1926–87), who managed to move fluidly between the worlds of style, film and art, mixing imagery magpie-like and inspiring New York's glitterati throughout the 1960s. Experimentation was the name of the game, with dresses made from paper, plastic and leatherette, in garish colours and pop-influenced psychedelic prints.*

A classic Warhol pose with silver hair and blank, enigmatic expression.

Throughout his life, Warhol was obsessed with fashion, and early on worked as a fashion illustrator for I. Miller Shoes as well as collaborating with designer Stephen Bruce, who produced dresses from fabric designed by Warhol in the early 1960s. By 1965 he had established the infamous Factory, an industrial loft with silver-coloured walls. He filled the building with celebrities and wannabes who dictated the tastes of New York for years, and at times the antics and clothes of his entourage were as much discussed as his art.

### Foiled again

Betsey Johnson (b. 1942) and Warhol were closely linked by a mutual love of experimentation. (It also helped that Johnson was married to John Cale, a member of The Velvet Underground, the hip New York band that was closely associated with the Factory.) Warhol was just mad about her trademark aluminium foil tank dresses. From 1965, she sold her clothes in a boutique called Paraphernalia, which was his image of fashion made flesh, featuring clothes made from plastics, paper, metals and even electric lights. Warhol's favourite colour – silver – was omnipresent. Johnson even designed a 'noise dress', which had loose grommets attached to the hem.

Is it a gas mask or does she plan to rob a bank? Johnson design.

**1965** Sonny and Cher's 'I Got You Babe' soars to the top of the American charts.

**1966** The Fair Packaging and Labeling Act in the US bans phony money-off and economy-size labels.

**1967** T-shirts proclaiming 'Che lives' become fashionable after the revolutionary Che Guevara is shot by government troops in Bolivia.

## SVENGALI OF STYLE

Warhol experimented with clothes as art, making dresses from his distinctive pop art prints – including S&H Green Stamps, Fragile and Brillo. The Factory look was influenced by the glamour of Hollywood movie stars: dresses were tight-fitting and worn with fur coats: earrings were enormous and makeup exaggerated. Factory members Edie Sedgwick and Baby Jane Holzer publicized the style and were frequently scrutinized in fashion magazines. At the centre of it all was Warhol himself, directing the group's every move.

His experimentation left a legacy for other designers. Halston *(see page 65)* used his distinctive flower screen-prints for dresses and scarves; *Stephen* SPROUSE (b. 1953) played with Warhol's camouflage paintings, as did *Anna Sui* (b. 1955). His dollar notes, Campbell's soup tin and banana screen-prints have covered countless T-shirts.

Mi-ao-w. A Warhol-inspired creation, just the thing to wear to cocktail parties in Beijing.

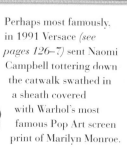

Perhaps most famously, in 1991 Versace *(see pages 126–7)* sent Naomi Campbell tottering down the catwalk swathed in a sheath covered with Warhol's most famous Pop Art screen print of Marilyn Monroe.

**1969** Manhattan button-maker N.G. Slater produces a range of buttons and appliqué motifs with smiley faces. In 1971 more than 20 million 'smile buttons' will be sold.

**1970** Tie-dyed fabrics, popularized by San Francisco hippies in the 60s, become high fashion when Halston designs blouses and scarves for his celebrity clientele.

**1971** George Harrison organises a Concert for Bangladesh, with Ravi Shankar, Ringo Starr and Eric Clapton.

## 1969~1975

# Hippiness Is . . .
## Flower power and psychedelic drugs

*In San Francisco in the 1960s they mixed a little Eastern philosophy, pacifism, poetry, rock music and hallucinogenic drugs, and came up with a brand new fashion style that remains influential more than twenty years on. Cheesecloth, love beads, kaftans and flares just keep floating back onto the catwalks.*

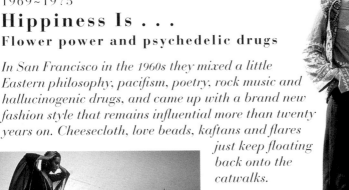

Thea Porter's 'just escaped from the harem' look of 1971.

John and Paul are obviously hippies, but who is that guy dressed as an undertaker?

The hippie movement can trace its roots to the idealistic commune living of the Haight-Ashbury district in San Francisco. Originally more concerned with alternative lifestyles than fashion, the first hippies rejected American consumerism and looked to the East for inspiration, travelling to Afghanistan and India in camper vans and picking up Buddhism and cult religious teachings like Hare Krishna along the way. It was perhaps inevitable that all this absorption of Eastern culture would engender an ethnic-inspired look with multi-coloured kaftans, Afghan coats, flower-power prints and symbols of peace being teamed with anti-fashion clothing like flared blue jeans, colourful multi-stranded beads, the

### Fashion's gypsy

Thea Porter (b. 1927) was born in Damascus, studied in London, moved to Beirut and set up a shop in London selling Turkish and Arabian textiles. By 1964 she had started to design clothing inspired by her travels and her elegant kaftans and ethnic prints fitted perfectly with the hippie demand for all things Eastern. Porter's look was extremely popular, with evening clothes made from chiffon, brocade and heavily-embroidered ethnic silks and velvets. She was also responsible for promoting that other key hippie look, the gypsy style, with full-skirted dresses, puffed sleeves and bodice detailing including keyhole cut-outs.

**1972** Tropical storm Agnes kills 134 people in the eastern US.

**1973** The longest solar eclipse in history can be seen from the southern Sahara Desert.

**1974** English gerontologist Alex Comfort writes *The Joy Of Sex*, which will become standard bedside reading for decades to come.

essential long, flowing hair, bare feet, army surplus, and home-made 'make do and mend' looks like patchwork and tie dye. Women also flirted with the nostalgia of a pre-industrial age, adopting romantic gypsy styles and the milkmaid smock pioneered by *Laura ASHLEY* (1925–85) – useful if you were overweight or pregnant.

By 1967 the Summer of Love was in full swing and hippie boutiques like 'I was Lord Kitchener's Valet' and 'Granny Takes A Trip' had sprung up in London. Drug culture was beginning to fuse with flower power and psychedelia started to make a big impact on hippie style, along with the unisex looks and bra-lessness that reflected the increased interest in the women's liberation movement.

Psychedelia had its roots firmly in the pop music of the time. Stars like Jimi Hendrix, Bob Dylan and Janis Joplin all did their bit for hippie style, with

## STYLE ICON
⭐

*Janis Joplin's powerful and passionate blues songs and her addiction to drink and drugs made her a cult figure for the hippie movement. Her songs, which include 'Ball And Chain' and 'Get It While You Can', were massive hits at the time and her personal style embodied the hippie rejection of the stereotyped feminine dolly-bird look, favouring androgynous waistcoats, velvet and the signature centre-parted hair. She died in 1970 from a heroin overdose.*

Janis does it her way – the original heroin chick.

Hendrix on a fashion trip in his bandleader's jacket, seeing the world through a purple haze.

skin-tight velvet trousers, abstract patterns and vivid colours inspired by tripping on LSD. The bold multi-coloured prints of *Emilio PUCCI* (1914–92) remain collectable today. However the early death of many icons, including Hendrix and Joplin, hastened the movement's demise as hippies grew up and instead of tuning in and dropping out, checked back in to the consumer society. The hippie style has continued to be influential with *Anna SUI* (b. 1955) showing hippie-look dresses in 1993 and Gucci resurrecting hippie-inspired embroidered blue jeans in 1999.

**1971** A man parachutes from a Boeing 727 with $200,000 ransom, after claiming his briefcase contains a bomb.

**1975** Tammy Wynette outrages feminists with her single 'Stand by Your Man'.

**1982** Liposuction is offered by European surgeons to suck away unwanted fat deposits.

1970s~1990s

# Exercise in Narcissism
## Aerobicswear

*On the fateful day when Jane FONDA (b. 1937) first encouraged her viewers to 'work that body' a new fashion legacy was born. Aerobics, and the ridiculous fashions it spawned during the mid 1980s, brought a new form of body consciousness into fashion, furthering the progress of performance sportswear towards becoming a wardrobe staple that could be worn beyond the mirrored walls and exercise bikes of the local health club – if you've got the figure for it.*

Putting the boot in: Nike flatten the competition in the field of trainers.

Aerobics wear was one of the first incarnations of what is now termed 'pro-active sportswear': garments that have been designed with active pursuits in mind, yet are equally appropriate as fashion items. In the 1985 film *Perfect*, John Travolta played an investigative journalist looking into the singles bar aspects of the gym scene, and although the camera spent the majority of the movie lingering over co-star Jamie Lee Curtis's leotard-clad form, the overwhelming message of the movie was that you no longer meet your partner under the church porch but drinking carrot juice in a health club suite (if you have a body like JLC).

Jamie Lee Curtis looking like a Lycra flamingo in the nauseating but influential *Perfect*.

### FASHION ESSENTIALS

Norma Kamali was the first designer to bring sweatshirt fabric from the baseball pitch to the high street (forget about nerdy students in sweatshirts with the name of their college on the front). In 1981 Karan launched a collection of 35 pieces made in sweatshirting, and now the tracksuit has become the 1990s equivalent of jeans and a denim jacket.

**1983** The film *Flashdance*, about a hopeful young dancer, launches a vogue for cut-away sweatshirts tight-fitting trousers and leg-warmers.

**1986** Nicotine chewing gum is introduced to help people quit the smoking habit.

**1989** A Dutch company makes a zip fastener 9,353 feet 8 inches long and lays it around the centre of Sneek. It has 2,565,900 teeth.

Today, advertising the body beautiful through sport is a growth area for the fashion industry, fusing advances in garment technology with marketing strategies that are now targeting groups such as the 'third-agers' (elderly people to you and me), vindicated by the 86-year-old woman who recently completed the London marathon. Relatively new sports such as windsurfing and snowboarding have spawned their own clothing industries, while the increased proportion of retired adults in the West has inspired a whole gamut of easy-care leisure clothes geared towards low-impact pursuits such as golf, bearing comforting brand names like Lady Augusta.

The symbiosis that exists between sport and fashion has had positive benefits for both industries. During the aerobics craze of the mid 1980s, American designers such as Donna Karan *(see page 104)* and *Norma KAMALI* (b. 1945) combined stretch with luxury fabrics to enable the newly toned to extol the virtues of exercise beyond the running machine. More recently Italian labels Prada and Miu Miu adopted rock-climbing trims and accessories that were better suited to an outdoor pursuits society than a gaggle of fashion editors. And Prada Sport, the

### Rubber stamp

Sportswear has come a long way since the day in 1971 when Nike co-founder Bill Bowerman poured liquid rubber onto a waffle iron as an aid to improving the performance of a training shoe. Today Nike revenues run into the billions and its Tokyo store took a million dollars in the first three days of trading. Yet many of the customers sporting the distinctive 'swoosh' logo *(see page 40)* may never have been near the sports track, as numerous beer bellies peering out below a sports-shirt testify.

diffusion line launched in 1997, is just one of a gamut of designer labels created to cash in on the sports and casualwear market. Conversely, the market for retro and vintage sportswear is a lucrative and growing market: limited edition sneakers can change hands for hundreds of pounds, and the importance of wearing the right training shoe is extremely well documented *(see page 41)*. No doubt Fonda's exhausting regimes have reduced the cellulite count in living rooms worldwide, but her real contribution to contemporary culture is the promotion of the body beautiful and the beginnings of the crossover between sport and fashion.

Jane Fonda demonstrates the importance of shaving.

**1950** When the US Public Health Service recommends that drinking water be fluoridated, the John Birch Society detects a Communist plot and mothers protest 'Forced medication is Un-American'.

**1951** Colour TV is introduced by CBS; those who can't afford it tape a rainbow-striped plastic sheet to their screen to reproduce the effect.

**1954** Marlon Brando is an ex-boxing champion turned docker fighting a corrupt labour boss in *On the Waterfront*. He wins an Oscar for the role.

1970s~90s

# The Four Marketeers
## American fashion

American genii.

*Fashion may have been created by the British, glamorized by the French and polished by the Italians, but it's marketed by the Americans, and none more so than the gods of Seventh Avenue in New York: Calvin KLEIN (b. 1942), Ralph LAUREN (b. 1939), Tommy HILFIGER (b. 1952) and Donna KARAN (b. 1948). None are creative geniuses and yet all four possess genius of a kind. Klein is a marketing genius; Lauren is a genius of interpretation; Hilfiger has revitalized the American preppie way-of-life; and Karan knew what working women wanted from their wardrobes.*

Each now heads up a company that is a commercial Goliath beyond the febrile world of fashion, managing diffusion lines, fragrances, accessories, and home furnishings. And yet, at the roots of each company is a driven personality from an ordinary background who has achieved the so-called American dream. Their success derives from the fact that each has exploited an idea to its apotheosis. Klein's use of sexuality in advertising goes beyond fashion to personify the morality of a decade. His revolutionary television ads featuring actress Brooke Shields, shot by photographer *Richard AVEDON* (b. 1923) in 1979–80, scandalized middle America.

More recently he thrust super-waif model Kate Moss *(see page 133)* into the league of the Supermodels by using her to advertise his fragrance Obsession; and after his use of rapper/actor Mark Wahlberg (aka Marky Mark; *see page 39*) to advertise underwear, no gay man would wear any other briefs.

Easy-to-wear: Karan's silk body and waist-pleated trousers, 1987.

Donna Karan's discovery was combining jersey with Lycra so as to appeal to women on the go. Her bodies and sarongs were integral to the body-consciousness of the late 1980s, while allowing the wearer a

**1959** Learning that 25 South African students have set a world record for the number of people who can fit into a phone box, American college students try to beat it.

**1960** US physicist Theodore Maiman comes up with the idea of the laser beam while waiting for a restaurant to open for breakfast.

**1963** The California skateboarding craze spreads across America; by 1965 over $30 million worth of skateboards will have been sold.

## FASHION ESSENTIALS

For that All-American look, try Calvin Klein's underpants for men and women and his sober, unisex clothes; Donna Karan's lycra bodysuits and wrap-around skirts in black, white, prune and grape; Ralph Lauren's hacking jackets, tailored shirts and crew necks; and Tommy Hilfiger's heavily logo-ed sportswear for homeboys and girls.

certain voluptuousness by hiding their worst features. One of her press releases famously proclaimed: 'You gotta accent your positive, delete your negative.' More lucrative for the company is the affordable DKNY collection, launched in 1988.

Hilfiger's 'All American' style is intrinsically home-spun with overt logos and a following among American youth; he was one of the first to target the considerable spending power of the Afro-Caribbean and Hispanic communities. He won the 'from the catwalk to the sidewalk' award at the first prestigious VH1 fashion awards in 1995, in celebration of the clothes most easily worn unaltered by the man and woman in the street. Today, Hilfiger's motivation is fuelled by the adage 'Tommy Rocks', which links the designer with music sponsorship deals such as his association with the Rolling Stones, his ultimate aim being world domination.

Ralph Lauren continues as the provider of classic good taste: he began as a tie salesman before launching the Polo brand *(see page 121)* and his company has

mushroomed ever since. They now occupy headquarters that have been panelled to resemble a baronial hall and a breathtaking range of products that even includes wallpapers and specially blended paints tinted to resemble vintage denim.

All four are icons of our times, and symbols of how publicity combined with a serviceable product can be marketed across the globe. As fellow American designer *Oscar de la Renta* (b. 1932) once put it: 'In Europe everyone raves about Prada and Gucci, but here in the States, once you go west of the Hudson River, nobody even knows who they are – it's Ralph, Calvin, Tommy and Donna.'

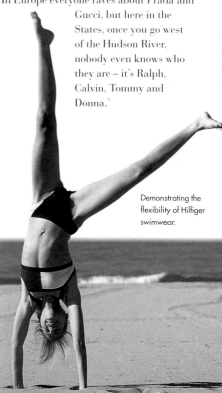

Demonstrating the flexibility of Hilfiger swimwear.

**1971** The phrase 'artificial intelligence' comes into use, denoting a machine that has human powers of reasoning.

**1979** Sony introduce the Walkman cassette player, which will annoy tube passengers for decades to come.

**1980** Kurosawa's *Kagemusha*, the tale of a 16th-century thief employed as the double of a clan leader, shares the Palme d'Or at Cannes with Bob Fosse's musical *All That Jazz*.

1970s~1990s

# Look to the Rising Sun

## Japanese design

The Emperor of Cool: Yamamoto takes a bow after a catwalk show.

*Swathed in layers of black shapeless silhouettes and extreme asymmetric cutting, the fashion mavens move in a gaggle like the Three Weird Sisters in* Macbeth. *They are wearing Yohji YAMAMOTO (b. 1943), one of the vanguard of Japanese designers who have gone some way to redefine our concepts of dress, imparting an oriental aesthetic that is in sharp contrast to Western traditions of cutting and construction.*

Miyake has trouble breathing (1982 design).

When Comme des Garçons, *Issey MIYAKE* (b. 1935) and Yohji Yamamoto first descended on Parisian catwalks during the early 1980s, their sexless, amorphous silhouettes were thrown down like a gauntlet against the prevailing mood of shoulder pads, ostentatious decoration and conspicuous consumption. They imparted an intellectualism to dress that seemed to endow fashion with a form of cerebral justification, despite the fact that many of their most alien ideas owed their origins to traditional Japanese clothing, such as the black robes of the farmer, the Samurai's armour or the Geisha's kimono. The critics loved it and today's devotees are more likely to be middle-aged women with a penchant for fine arts than dumb blondes (a dress cut like a sack won't show off a pair of silicone implants to best advantage).

After their initial success prompted by the 'shock of the new', fashion watchers recognized a creativity and lack of compromise from the Japanese that could

Not an outfit from 'Doctor Who' – one of Miyake's pleated creations.

**1983** Chicago motorists can chat on cellular car phones after Motorola set up a series of transmitters throughout the city and a computer system to forward calls to cars.

**1986** Nintendo is launched in the US with games like 'The Legend of Zelda', and first-year sales top $300 million.

**1999** NATO accidentally bombs the Chinese Embassy in Belgrade.

only be admired. Yamamoto's approach explores asymmetry and an appreciation of the irregular for its lack of artifice and proximity to nature. Likewise, the mantra of Comme des Garçons designer *Rei KAWAKUBO* (b. 1942) combines the essence of traditional work-end street-wear with an understanding of *wabi sabi*, the Japanese aesthetic principle of beauty imperfect. Issey Miyake is best known for his pleated garments that appear in both his mainline collections and less expensive 'Pleats Please' range, both of which have the ability to transmogrify the body into a radical form of sculpture or a column of blank textured colour. Comme des Garçons' extreme aesthetic has taken the rejection of convention

## FASHION ESSENTIALS

Miyake's rattan body sculptures of 1982 created a sartorial exoskeleton that was immediately hailed as visionary and his pleated look has been widely copied. Comme des Garçon's knits of the mid 1980s were designed on a knitting machine that had been deliberately mis-programmed to produce holes and ladders. Yamamoto's ragged hems and worn-out aesthetic were a direct reaction to the tidal wave of consumer products that enveloped Japan in the 1950s; he swathes the body in voluminous fabrics that often have added pockets and straps.

Kabuki theatre influences evening wear (1977).

### The scent of ozone

'Eau D'Issey', introduced in 1993 by Miyake, was the first fragrance to capitalize on the newly developed 'ozonic' note; more recently Comme des Garçons has produced 'Odeur 53', which includes the self-consciously synthetic notes of fresh laundry and burnt rubber, and entirely rejects the notion that perfumes require a basis in floral or natural essences.

and consumer culture one step further through its flagship retail outlets, designed with architect Takao Kawasaki: the clothes are hidden behind frosted glass screens from all but the most assiduous shopper, and unsold stock is rumoured to be burnt at the season's end.

All three design clothes that mutate the body, covering and disguising the torso. They pioneered ideas of deconstruction *(see pages 134–5)* before the Belgian designers, made black the fashion staple it has become today, without funereal or cocktail associations, and, due to a carefully cultivated inscrutability, after nearly twenty years at the pinnacle of fashion they retain an aura of mystique that the West has never fully penetrated.

**1970** The Velvet Underground, featuring Lou Reed and John Cale, break up. An attempted reunion in the 1990s ends in acrimony.

**1971** A Canadian TV station buys 1,144 episodes of 'Coronation Street'. To watch them all would take 20 days, 15 hours and 44 minutes.

**1974** A fireball 10,000 times brighter than a full Moon is photographed over Sumava, Czechoslovakia.

## 1970~1980
# Punk Revolution
### Bondage and safety pins

*Punk defined itself as an anti-fashion statement. The music was harsh and raw, the clothes – aimed at the unemployed, school leavers and students – were made from cheap and readily available fabrics. But the movement that started as a form of rebellion became one of Britain's strongest cultural influences in the 1970s.*

I am the Anti-Creased: Johnny Rotten, Sid Vicious & co promote anarchy in the UK fashion world.

Thrift shop clothes were slashed and reconstructed, tights were laddered, school uniforms were bastardized. Everyday items like safety pins, razors and tampons were subverted in an attempt to shock the establishment. Piercing was big news, with safety pins through noses, ears and cheeks, while makeup was taken to new extremes, influenced by tribal painting and vintage horror films. Hair was soaped, spiked and shaved, with the distinctive Mohican becoming the favourite crop.

Plastic fantastic: Westwood's bondage collection had its devotees.

Punk music was influenced by David Bowie and the New York Dolls, but it took promoter and ultimate style exploiter Malcolm McLaren and his designer and partner *Vivienne WESTWOOD* (b. 1941) to fully publicize the new movement. In the 1970s their shop on London's King's Road went through a series of metamorphoses, from 'Let it Rock' in 1971 to the cult 'Sex' in 1974, and later 'Seditionaries'. 'Sex' became world-famous for Westwood's collection of bondage-style clothing featuring mainly black outfits that were buckled, split, slashed, strapped and chained

**1975** Martin Amis, song of Kingsley, writes *Dead Babies*.

**1976** Abba have three massive hits this year with 'Mamma Mia', 'Fernando' and 'Dancing Queen'.

**1977** Britons celebrate the Queen's Silver Jubilee with street parties; a few protest by playing the Sex Pistols' tribute single 'God Save the Queen' or wearing 'Sod the Jubilee' T-shirts.

## STYLE ICON
★

*Jordan became a symbol of what it meant to be Punk. She wore suspenders and transparent net skirts to school before being suspended and worked briefly for Harrods, where she painted her face green. She commuted every day from Brighton in full Punk gear complete with Mohican and starkly painted face to work in 'Sex'. Jordan was the perfect example of Punk's anti-beauty ethos and her distinctive style soon ensured that she was photographed by David Bailey and cast in the Punk film* Jubilee *(1977). She set up a company called 'Deadly Feminine' selling her own designs and made occasional appearances with the band Adam & the Ants.*

### English eccentric

The signature of all Vivienne Westwood collections is meticulous research and the fact that no one can ever guess what she'll come up with next. Her initial bondage collection mixed sado-masochistic equipment with her own very particular (some would say peculiar) take on sex, and she has continued to be a strong and credible voice for street culture, consistently ahead of the field with innovations like her Pirate collection (1981) which heralded New Romanticism *(see pages 118–19)*. Other influential collections have included Witches (1983) with its nylon macs and trainers; the 1985 mini-crinolines, bustles and corsets; the 1987 Harris tweed collection; her 1989 nude dress with fig leaf; and the legendary platform shoes that Naomi Campbell fell off in 1993. She was crowned British Designer of the Year for two years running (1990 and 1991) and launched her own perfume in 1989, in a bottle topped with a regal orb. Long live Queen Viv!

designer *Zandra RHODES* (b. 1940) was producing sanitized versions of the slashed and safety-pinned outfits (with a bit of diamanté added for good measure), forever robbing punk of its initial power to shock. The 1990s Goth look, characterized by black clothes, stiffly spiked hair, panda eyes and deathly white makeup, was a later incarnation with a bit of heavy metal thrown in.

A courting couple display their multicoloured plumage in one of their natural habitats – a CND rally in a London park, 1983.

(and virtually impossible to walk in). The collection was worn by the Sex Pistols on and off stage. 'Sex' also sold the definitive Punk T-shirts designed to offend, featuring slogans on anarchy, paedophilia and pornography along with anti-religious and anti-monarchy images.

Ironically, Punk's anti-fashion stance became a victim of its own success as it was absorbed into popular culture. By 1979,

**1971** Many Christians believe if you play Led Zeppelin's song 'Stairway to Heaven' backwards you hear satanic incantations.

**1973** For one show Gary Glitter wears platform boots that are nearly 6 feet tall.

**1977** The Pompidou Centre in Paris opens, with all its pipes, ducts and lifts on the outside of the building. Critics say it looks like a sewage plant but the public love it.

1970s~1990s

# Bad Taste

## Those guilty wardrobe secrets

Flarey nice: a scary denim playsuit, circa 1973. Imagine bumping into him on a dark night . . .

*Fashion, like taste, is relative: that lime green Lycra mini-dress you bought at Christmas is now languishing with dozens of its siblings on the sale rail, and the purple bouclé suit that looked fantastic when your friend borrowed it the weekend before, casts a death-like pallor on your skin. Some clothes are desirable on a supermodel but in reality are better off in the bin, and to make matters worse the fashion system itself perpetuates the idea of bad taste, by encouraging the consumer to enter a continuing cycle of purchase and disposal rather than end up looking out-of-date.*

> **STYLE ICON** ★
>
> *They may have celebrity – but boy do they dress badly! Elton John, Fergie, Celine Dion, Kate Winslet, Cher, Mary J. Blige, The Artist Formerly known As Prince, Chelsea Clinton, Zsa Zsa Gabor, Woody Allen, Cherie Blair, and all boy bands. I could go on.*

As fashions change, so do our tastes: when a style gets too commonplace, as in the current case of army trousers, it becomes anathema. Those who were proud to sport a pair of baggy fatigues at a pop festival six months ago will avoid them like the plague after their grandmother has invested in a pair to be worn on the golf course. If you are a hoarder, five minutes' delving into the darkest recesses of your wardrobe will provide ample memories of sartorial mistakes that are best forgotten. Every decade has its own fashion faux pas – those garments that were once de rigeur and are now deemed so dire that their only outings are to fancy dress parties or the charity shop (there's always some poor soul who'll snap up items that have become laughable a decade after they were bought).

**1981** More than 300 people are eaten by piranhas when a boat sinks near Obidos, Brazil.

**1985** British fashion designer Laura Ashley dies, but the floral print frocks live on.

**1989** The world's tallest sand sculpture is built in Japan. It is 56 feet 2 inches tall and is called 'Invitation to Fairyland'.

However, today's dissemination of style has decreed that there is very little that will not appeal to someone somewhere. Buzz words like 'kooky' and 'kitsch' have encouraged hordes of teenage girls to mix ostensibly hideous charity shop finds with garish plastic jewellery and items designed to appeal to the under-fives. This cutsie hybridization of style evolved into a new sub-culture that has now won a type of fashion credibility. A case in point is that of the Milanese design house Prada *(see pages 128–9)*, a company so successful at re-combining imagery from the past that it has been able to re-merchandise the self-same product to the customer who would balk at the original. For the Prada-wearing devotee, the nylon shirt that looks like 1970s wallpaper or a grey flannel pinafore reminiscent of an old secondary-school

Flower power comes around again? Or did they just have a fight with some dreadful old curtains?

uniform, may owe their origins to the worst excesses of bad taste, and yet, with the stamp of designer approbation, they suddenly become high fashion once again.

Deely-boppers: fine if you are ten, but just plain silly on anyone older.

## FASHION ESSENTIALS

Here are some suggestions, should you wish to advertise your bad taste:

☞ Stock up on pastel-coloured shell suits *(see page 123)*, now the butt of comedians;

☞ Get some deely-boppers, those extended antennae that automatically lower the IQ on application;

☞ Breast implants are currently deemed incredibly poor taste, damaging to health and credibility;

☞ Rainbow leg-warmers, funky in the mid 1980s, are now the stuff of children's TV presenters;

☞ Blazers with enormous shoulder pads *(see page 122)* are ideal for extras on Dynasty but dodgy for anyone else.

**1973** Wayne Sleep enters the record books after performing an *entrechat* (crossing and uncrossing his legs five times in midair) in just 0.71 seconds.

**1978** Tom Robinson's single 'Glad to be Gay' is banned by the BBC.

**1980** The film *Cruising*, starring Al Pacino, is attacked by gay rights activists for its stereotypical characters.

1970s~present

# The Body Beautiful
## Gay fashion

Hello there, handsome.

*Gay fashion can easily be pigeonholed as a synthesis of the campest, the most provocative and the most clichéd aspects of men's and (in the case of drag queens) women's sexuality. It can carry with it a code of ethics and behaviour or simply display a six-pack buffed and toned by numerous visits to the gym. But although straight society would never outwardly acknowledge it, gay fashion has an enormous influence on the way we all dress today.*

Without too much sociological dissection, gay men and women use fashion as a way of underlining their identity in a celebration of being different. It is a fashion of combination and appropriation. Protective biker leathers are transformed into fetishistic harnesses and symbols of masculinity; army surplus is more often seen on a dance floor than an assault course; and the thermal T-shirt is less about preventing chilblains and more to do with attracting admiring glances.

Gay fashion is also about hedonism. Look in any gay man's bathroom cabinet and it will be replete with potions and fragrances that put a beauty counter to shame. While Mr and Mrs Average are contending with messy toddlers, whites stained pink in the washing machine and the occasional game of squash after a day at the office, their gay counterparts are

**1985** Actor Rock Hudson dies of AIDS after being the first public figure in the US to admit he is suffering from the disease.

**1994** British MPs vote to cut the age of consent for gay sex from 21 to 18.

**1997** Tony Mattia of Brighton has to move into a bigger home to make room for his collection of 900 Barbie dolls. He changes their clothes once a month.

shopping in designer outlets and pumping their pecs in the pursuit of beauty, rather than trying to prevent middle-aged spread.

Of course, this is a huge generalization, but there are vast cultural and financial differences in the way straight and non-straight society makes their sartorial decisions. Many designers are gay and, like the birth of disco music in the gay clubs of the 1970s, trends that begin within the gay community are soon assimilated into mainstream society. Even drag queens, once the bastion of middle-aged men dressed in a parody of womenswear, are likely to be as glamorous as any supermodel today. And if you don't believe me, ask any designer who buys the most outrageous pieces in a couture collection – it's just as likely to be a Mexican transsexual as a society matron.

Inevitably gay fashion is pigeonholed into the clichés that once personified it. Not all lesbians wear dungarees and checked shirts, and most gay men would cringe at the thought of dressing like the Village People or Julian Clary. In fact, everyday items such as army

'Macho Man', 'YMCA' and 'In the Navy': remember those pop classics by the Village People?

trousers, moisturizers for men, and a body beautiful style of fitted dressing have become integral within both gay and straight society. But no prizes for guessing where they originated.

What a drag: fetching fishtail frock with huge puff sleeves.

### FASHION ESSENTIALS

Although all but redundant except among the most traditional members of the gay community, the hanky code is a way for gay men to show their sexual preferences through the discreet positioning of a coloured handkerchief in the back pocket of their trousers; its colour and position denotes the wearer's sexual persuasion and/or proclivities. Here are explanations of just a few of the more obscure shades on offer:

☞ Pale yellow: (on left) spits; (on right) drools
☞ Lavender: (on left) likes drag queens; (on right) drag queen
☞ White velvet: (on left ) voyeur (on right) will put on a show
☞ Teddybear : (on left ) cuddler; (on right) cudlee
☞ Houndstooth: (on left) likes to nibble; (on right) will be bitten
☞ Silver lamé: (on left) wants sex with a celebrity; (on right) a celebrity
☞ Brown corduroy: (on left) headmaster; (on right) student
☞ Coral: (on left) suck my toes; (on right) I'll suck yours
☞ Apricot: (on left) two tons o'fun; (on right) chubby chaser
and so on....

**1970** Conservationists win the battle to prevent a major new airport being built in Florida's Everglades.

**1973** More than 50% of Americans believe in UFOs and 10% claim to have seen one.

**1979** The world's first 'Green' political party is founded by Petra Kelly in Germany.

## 1970s~1990s
# 'I'd Rather Go Naked'
### Fashions in fur

*It may have been OK for Raquel Welch to sport a fur bikini in the film* One Million Years BC *(1966), but wear an animal skin today, whether it be mammoth or sable, and you're likely to get attacked in the street, especially if you live in the UK or US. Fur is now an emotive issue; wearing it in some countries is anathema, yet in others it remains a status symbol. In Spain and Italy, it is commonplace to see women of a certain age taking their customary evening stroll clad in a menagerie of skins, some in old-fashioned movie-starlet styles, others in the latest designs from master furriers such as Fendi (see box).*

**Famous fur wearers**
HM Queen Elizabeth II and her Mum; Margaret Thatcher; Elizabeth Taylor (in the Burton years); Eartha Kitt; Naomi Campbell. Campaigners say it takes two hundred dumb animals to make a fur coat but only one to wear it.

Of course they wore fur in the Stone Age. They had bouffant hairstyles as well, I expect.

Wonder what you could make out of Anna Wintour's famous bob?

Ironically, it is the northern countries that are most ardently anti-fur. In London no department store dare sell the stuff and in the US, pro-fur American

*Vogue* editor Anna Wintour had a corpse of the non-edible kind dropped in her lap at a posh New York eaterie. PETA (People for the Ethical Treatment of Animals) is a major force in the anti-fur lobbying movement, attracting supermodels including Christy Turlington, Tyra Banks and Marcus Schenkenberg to pose in its provocative 'I'd Rather Go Naked Than Wear Fur' advertising campaigns. In the UK, photographer David Bailey (b. 1938) made a dramatic advert featuring a catwalk model swinging a fur coat and spraying the audience with blood.

**1984** The movie *Gremlins* features malevolent little furry creatures terrorizing human beings.

**1987** The black gollywogs in Enid Blyton's 'Noddy' stories are replaced by gnomes, in the interests of political correctness.

**1989** At an auction house in London, an American collector buys a German-made Steiff teddy-bear for $88,000.

While campaigning organizations such as PETA have been responsible for the closure of numerous fur farms and the exposure of cruel practices, such as injecting minks with weed killer and electronically inducing heart attacks in perfectly healthy animals, the world fur industry continues blithely to furnish the fashion trade with pelts of all shapes and sizes. According to the Canadian Fur Council, the fur trade accounts for only 0.25 percent of the animals used in North America for food, clothing and other purposes each year and it claims that twice as many unwanted pets are destroyed in humane shelters, yet fur is still deemed unwarrantable by most American women.

Conversely, in Europe fur is experiencing somewhat of a fashion renaissance. Initially it reappeared as a trim on collars and cuffs, which campaigners claimed was an insidious attempt to reintroduce animal skins through the 'back door'; more recently real furs have been treated to look fake through re-dyeing (now what's the point of that?). It seems that for some people fashion's current obsession with luxury is beginning to override any concern about animal welfare. Perhaps British design duo Copperwheat Blundell have got the solution to this age old problem sorted out once and for all: instead of using real animal fur, they purchased a batch of human hair from a wig factory to make their cozy winter coats and dresses, allowing the wearer to counter any criticism with the riposte: 'No, actually it's human…'

Naomi Campbell models Fendi furs after taking part in the 'I'd Rather Go Naked' campaign.

**1977** Students lead protests against magazines that exploit women.

**1984** The new Staatsgalerie in Stuttgart is made from stone, glass and coloured metal, and is described as 'more a landscape than a building.'

**1992** In Germany, Neo-Nazi skinheads are responsible for more than 2,280 racial attacks.

1977~present

# The Avant-garde Businessman

## Helmut Lang

Lang's army-surplus style made up in luxurious fabrics.

*The work of Austrian designer Helmut LANG (b. 1956) acts as a barometer of the way we perceive fashion in the late 1990s. He has been successively accredited with popularizing deconstruction (see pages 134-5), futurism (see pages 138-9) and minimalism (see pages 106-7). He is probably one of the most tacitly emulated designers working today, and a carefully cultivated mystique has added to the adoration he receives from the press, who dare not criticize something they don't fully understand.*

> **FASHION ESSENTIALS**
>
> Sombre colours with a bright flash; quality fabrics; uneven seams and edges; perfectly fitting shift dresses and jackets; army surplus re-cut in luxury fabrics; down-filled jackets; paint-splattered jeans.

Lang began designing in 1977 then decamped his shows to Paris in the mid 1980s, where his low-key aesthetic was in radical contrast to the prevailing shoulderpads and aggressive ostentation. His early collections, now veiled in the mists of fashion mythology, retained a Teutonic dressiness, which has subsequently been eclipsed by his reputation for stark modern wearability. His knack of appropriating -fashion classics such as army surplus page 28) for a designer-literate clientele nitized basic garments by executing luxury fabrics, more suited to an outique than a pop festival.

Lang's contribution to contemporary fashion is about twisting the accepted into the challenging: he popularised stretch T-shirts in the early 1990s, making thermal cool. His use of radically synthetic fabrics such as Aertex, stretch lace and rip-stop nylon have given humble fabrics a new credibility, and his pared-down silhouettes always contain a disturbing quirk that updates a simple item – such as a shift

**1993** President Clinton's plane holds up traffic in LA airport for forty minutes while he has his hair cut by a Beverly Hills stylist.

**1994** Egyptian novelist Nnguib Mahfouz is stabbed in the neck by a militant Islamic fundmentalist in Cairo; he survives.

**1999** Environmentalists pull up genetically modified crops in protests across the UK.

## The Webbed catwalk

Inseparable from Lang's genius as a designer are his marketing methods. His fashion shows are legendarily basic, swift and unpretentious, as models move through brightly lit rooms at a phenomenal pace. His guest lists are notoriously small. For every journalist basking under the halogen lights beside the minuscule catwalk, there are another five shivering on the pavement outside, desperately trying to persuade the heavies on the door to let them enter. Sometimes he has rejected shows altogether, choosing to show his designs on the Internet (www.helmutlang.com), thereby acknowledging the power of the Worldwide Web to disseminate visual information globally seconds after it has taken place *(see page 19.)*

Lang is known for unusual combinations of fabrics: sheer and opaque, shiny and matt, cheap and pricey.

Lang's pink chiffon dress was much copied in the high street.

dress with a hanging sleeve like a bandage, or an irregular seam running across a chiffon top like a bright pink cicatrice. And yet, as avant-garde as his designs might be, it's very rare that they are unwearable; rather, they encapsulate the synthesis of the zeitgeist – resolutely modern but always resolutely commercial.

Nowadays Lang is not just a leader of the avant-garde but also a real world-class commercial power. His recent move to show in New York has placed him among the big league of designers. His more affordable jeans line has up to 700 stockists worldwide and newly forged manufacturing links with an Italian design house have opened his market potential even further. Mooted as a successor for the mantle of Armani or Calvin Klein for the new century, Lang's story is by no means finished. He has won the hearts of the fashion cognoscenti; now it's time to persuade the general public.

| **1980** Mount St Helen's erupts in Washington and the entire north side of the volcano collapses into a river of lava. | **1981** The musical *March of the Falsettos* opens in New York and runs for 170 performances. | **1982** Dustin Hoffman plays a man pretending to be a woman in *Tootsie* and Julie Andrews plays a woman pretending to be a man playing a woman in *Victor/Victoria*. |
| --- | --- | --- |

## 1980~1985
# Gender Bender
## Playing with sexual stereotypes

*In 1983 the Sun newspaper coined the phrase 'gender bender' as a label for those who experiment with the boundaries of male/female dressing, hair and makeup. Of course, some had always enjoyed this predilection but it became a popular street style in the early 1980s alongside the New Romantic movement. Now you could get your summer togs from a fancy-dress shop rather than M & S.*

Adam Ant mixes Native American with 19th-century military looks.

Started in London clubs like Blitz and St Moritz, the new mood took the hard edge off Punk and created a form of dressing that was far more theatrical, narcissistic and playful. *Vivienne WESTWOOD* (b. 1941) was responsible for dressing Adam & the Ants in foppish, Regency-inspired attire, then her Pirate collection in 1981 spearheaded a layered, androgynous look.

Other themes quickly developed, including preening dandies, dreadlocks and even Hasidic Jew ringlets and hats. London clubs became the stage for outrageous scenes of dressing up and visual experimentation with designers including *David HOLAH* (b. 1958) and *Stevie STEWART* (b. 1958) of Body Map fame experimenting with ruffles, frills and Lycra. New Romantic singers included

Steve Strange (who cited David Bowie's transsexual experiments as a huge influence), Spandau Ballet, Duran Duran and cult gender bender *BOY GEORGE* (b. 1961). George's blatant sexually ambivalent style of dress became a national obsession. After appearing in cult magazine *I-D* wearing a nun's habit, he traversed the whole gamut of styles before arriving at the look that initially baffled

Westwood's swashbuckling attiire sported by model Nadja Auermann.

**1983** Culture Club's 'Karma Chameleon' is UK hit of the year and Boy George's pigtails, dress and makeup receive much press attention.

**1984** James F. Fixx, author of *A Complete Guide to Running*, dies of a heart attack while out running.

**1985** The Church of England allows women to be ordained as deacons for the first time.

## Total Fashion Victim

Designer Stephen Linard was certainly in the right place at the right time, sharing a squat in London with Boy George before graduating from the fashion course at St Martin's College in 1981 with a collection called Reluctant Emigrés. His trademark pieces anticipated the New Romantic look, with organza and astrakhan coats and images culled from priests and popes. He also acted as a front man for the aptly named fashion-based club, Total Fashion Victim. His contemporaries catering for pop star tastes included Helen Robinson of PX, Christopher and Susan Brick of Demob, and Stephen Jones for hats (*see page 47*).

Boy George famously quipped that he'd rather have a cup of tea than sex.

### STYLE ICON
★

One half of the cult 1980s band Eurythmics, Scottish singer **Annie Lennox** (b. 1954) proved that it was possible to gender bend in reverse when she stormed the charts with 'Sweet Dreams Are Made Of This' in 1983. Lennox's androgynous appearance was as much talked about as Boy George's. She explained: 'I wanted to reinvent myself so it was natural for me to wear more mannish clothes because it gave me more power.' In her pinstripe suits and ties, with her cropped orange hair and sharp bone structure, she became the epitome of the female gender bender. However, her look was seen more in magazines than on the streets, being less acceptable and harder-edged than Boy George's feminine image.

viewers when he appeared on 'Top of The Pops' with Culture Club in 1982. His makeup, hats, ringlets and tunics emblazoned with stars of David and Ethiopian flags were copied slavishly, particularly by female fans. In the tabloids, endless column inches were devoted to George and fellow gender bender Marilyn (so called because of his uncanny resemblance to Marilyn Monroe) until their fall from grace and favour.

Skirts for men were introduced by Body Map and Jean-Paul Gaultier (*see page 95*), among others. They never really caught on down the rugby club but you'll still see the odd pop star sporting a nifty wraparound (Michael Hutchence was keen on them) and footballer David Beckham loves slinking around with his Posh Spice in flowery sarong.

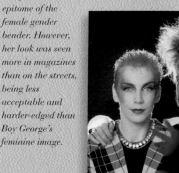

Sweet Dreams: Annie proves that girls can be boys.

FASHION ~ A CRASH

**1980** Young journalist Lisa Birnbach launches a craze for conservative chic in the US with *The Official Preppy Handbook*; over a million copies are sold.

**1984** The first Virgin Atlantic flight from London to New York costs £99 for a single fare.

**1987** Kellogg's introduce a new cereal called Just Right, containing raisins, nuts and dates.

1980~present

# Brands Mean Business
## Selling dreams through designer names

Tommy Hilfiger can sell you the clothes, but not the face, figure or hair.

*Branding is not just about sticking a designer name on a pair of jeans and hoping that the public will buy them; it's about selling a dream lifestyle in the shape of a product. (Yes, you too can live in a stylish warehouse apartment, have millions of cool friends, drive the latest sports car and sleep with drop-dead-gorgeous models.) Top designers are willing to plough literally millions into marketing campaigns to sell their dream effectively. Not surprisingly, branding kings tend to be American and the areas where branding works best are with products which manage to encompass the wannabe desire of the public for a certain brand but are sold at a popular price. Perfume, underwear and diffusion lines are obvious examples and the key word here is 'aspirational'. What brand are you?*

Is that a gun in your pocket? Don Johnson's Bossy image.

**B**rands are vital to the international success of designers. The average ~nue that comes from haute couture is less than ten percent of the designer's ~rofits and most of their money is ~m branding and licensing. Clever ~lacement is a favoured way of brands and designers fight to ~lothing ranges to films and

**1988** 'Neighbours' is the UK's third most popular TV show and Kylie Minogue sings 'I Should Be So Lucky'.

**1990** French and British construction workers digging the Channel Tunnel finally meet in the middle.

**1995** The Levi's 501 drugstore advert wins 33 awards this year.

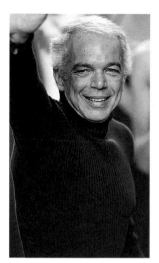

Ralph Lauren: even his armpit is aristocratic.

## Snob values

If the designer's name has the potential power to sell everything from belts to sunglasses on an international scale, then the best way to maximize on market potential can be to license the name to a range of manufacturers. Carefully monitored, licensing is an effective and extremely lucrative way of promoting a brand but caution has to be exercised, and control maintained over quality and marketing. Overuse of a designer name can lead to a lack of exclusivity and consequent devaluation of the brand. In the 1980s Pierre Cardin had awarded over 800 licenses including, bizarrely, one for scuba-diving equipment. Other companies, such as Hermès, prefer to retain tight control over licensing, only working with its own workshop to ensure that the brand doesn't become too common, darling.

which by the mid 1980s had got completely out of hand. It was estimated that 90 percent of all the Louis Vuitton bags seen on the streets were inferior copies. Although the situation is marginally better now, due to tighter controls and ruthless protectionist policies, the pull of the brand will always be powerful enough to ensure there are profits in piracy.

### STYLE ICON
★

*American designer **Ralph Lauren** (b. 1939) (see also page 104) was quick to appreciate the boundless possibilities of selling not just clothes but a whole lifestyle to his customers. He reworked themes from the 1930s and 1940s, designed classic American-style sportswear and spent a fortune on beautifully shot, glossy advertising campaigns that encapsulated his idealized view of East Coast American aristocracy (think beach-house and yacht on Martha's Vineyard). He also sensibly promoted his polo player emblem and created an easily recognizable status symbol that people are only too happy to pay a premium for, especially if they don't know a polo stick from a pogo stick.*

popular TV series; for example, the use of Hugo Boss clothing in series like 'Miami Vice' and 'Dynasty' helped to ensure the international status of the German company.

However, developing a brand is not for the faint-hearted. It is estimated that seventeen out of every twenty new brands die a quick and expensive death. Ironically, one of the most effective ways of judging the success of a brand is to calculate how much it is copied illegally. Top names like Chanel, Ralph Lauren Polo, Armani, Gucci, Calvin Klein, Versace, Hermès and Prada have all fallen prey to a vast industry of counterfeit goods,

**1981** American TV soap 'Dynasty' will popularise ranges of clothing and luggage, as well as the 'Krystle' and 'Scoundrel' perfumes evoking the two female leads.

**1986** Prince Charles admits on British television that he talks to plants.

**1987** In the film *Wall Street* Michael Douglas proclaims that 'Greed is good' and 'Lunch is for wimps'.

1980s

# Consumer Excess
## Shoulder pads and shell suits

*When British designer Katherine* HAMNETT *(b. 1948) claimed responsibility for the term 'power dressing', she was referring not only to the inexorable rise of women in the workplace but also to the*

Big hair, big head.

*American baseball shoulder that came to personify the aggressive fashions of the mid 1980s. 'Dynasty'-style dressing was not the only legacy from the decade that taste forgot; we used so much hairspray that the ozone layer became severely depleted and enough blue eyeshadow to rival the best Russian air hostesses.*

T o understand the truly horrific styles of the 1980s, one must analyze the motivation that begot items like multi-coloured leg warmers, parachute pants and pastel suit jackets. We were in the midst of an economic boom after the doldrums of the late 1970s; Thatcherism and Reaganomics, privatization and the mantra 'greed is good' inspired a new form of ostentation that was all about the 'body beautiful' and if your figure was less than perfect you could hide it under a pile of junk jewellery or a baggy shirt cinched to

the waist with a wide elastic belt. At the designer level of the market, *Claude* MONTANA (b. 1949) showed shoulders wide enough to balance a cup of tea on and German label Mondi carved a niche for itself with ostentatious

**1988** According to an ex-White House chief of staff, Ronald Reagan consults an astrologer before making important decisions – like the dates to hold nuclear arms limitation talks with Mikhail Gorbachev.

**1989** British teenagers are taking Ecstasy, dancing to acid house and attending raves, wearing baggy sportswear with touches of hippie psychedelia.

**1990** Yuppie flu is the trendy disease of the year, affecting people in highly pressurised jobs.

blazers complete with fake naval insignia and gold buttons. If you were a bloke, pastel suiting inspired by the TV series 'Miami Vice' looked great under the soft light of the Florida Keys, but not so effective in a Basildon wine bar.

In retrospect, 1980s fashions were influenced more by the media than the power of the international catwalks. Katherine Hamnett's visit to 10 Downing Street wearing a '58% Don't Want Pershing' (missiles) T-shirt did more than confound the then Prime Minister Margaret Thatcher, but spawned a slew of copies from contemporary pop icons. If you were a teenager during the decade, odds-on you possessed either a 'Choose Wham' or a 'Frankie Says...' sweatshirt. Parents started wearing brighter colours in the guise of cerise and mint casualwear,

## Teen flicks

In America, the re-birth of the teen movie influenced sartorial decisions: Molly Ringwald's hand-me-down style in *Pretty in Pink* (1986) and Madonna's screen debut in *Desperately Seeking Susan* (1985) encouraged girls to slap on the junk jewellery and team tutus with leggings, while their opposite sex wore tightly buttoned shirts, bolero jackets and even diamanté for the bravest boys willing to risk raised eyebrows on the last bus home. The Brat Pack have a lot to answer for.

Molly Ringwald wears her grandma's cast-offs in *Pretty In Pink*.

Krystle and Alexis remind us how vulgar 'Dy–nasty' really was.

that culminated in the worst fashion mistake of the late 1980s – the shell suit – reviled when it was discovered that many were not just sweaty but also inflammable. Sadly, the caring-sharing 1990s preoccupation with ecology and natural fibres put paid to the exuberant bad taste of the 1980s. Armani's subtle suiting and the popularity of a Zen-like minimalism in dress consigned the leg-warmer and the rah-rah skirt to the dustbin, and despite recent efforts to revive the shoulder pad, you are only likely to find them in thrift shops and at provincial wedding receptions these days.

**1980** Gwen Matthewman of West Yorkshire attains the world record for being the fastest knitter, at a speed of 111 stitches per minute.

**1981** Italy's cabinet resigns after 953 government officials are linked to a secret masonic organisation.

**1986** The Russian space station Mir is launched into orbit; it will suffer various accidents, including a collision with a supply vessel in 1997.

1980s~present
# King of the Soft Shoulder
## Giorgio Armani

*King of the unstructured suit and emperor of understatement, Italian designer Giorgio ARMANI (b. 1934) is one of the most influential creative talents of our day. The soft-shouldered suits he popularized during the mid 1980s have come to underpin fashion in the late 20th century and his impact is supreme, his name in Italy revered as much as the Pope's. Visitors to his headquarters in Milan can't help noticing the Emporio Armani illuminated hangar at the local airport.*

Lounge-lizard smile and year-round tan: the godfather of fashion.

Armani gets into men's underwear (1996).

Unlike most of today's design heros, who are swept by a tide of hyperbole onto the pages of the glossies with little or no track record, Armani began his apprenticeship with the Italian store group Rinoscente in 1954, initially working as a window dresser. After seven years in the company's design department, he graduated to creating menswear for *Nino Cerrutti* (b. 1930) before launching his own menswear label in 1974, followed by womenswear a year later. Now at the helm of the biggest-selling European designer label in the US, Armani's ethos has altered little since his first soft-shouldered jackets in the mid 1980s. His formula was simple: rather than construct a jacket according to conventional tailoring principles, the Armani silhouette draped from the

**1988** Jasper Johns's sculpture *False Start* – in which he stencilled labels over painted objects – is sold for a record $17.05 million.

**1991** *The Big Issue* magazine is founded in London, produced and sold by the homeless.

**1996** European couples have an average of 1.5 children, while those in the Middle East and Africa have 6.

Jodie Foster favours Armani suits for business meetings and picking up Oscars.

### FASHION ESSENTIALS

Never one for brash colours or bold prints, the Armani palette is typified by quiet colors such as taupe, olive, fawn and camel. His suits have relaxed shoulders, uncluttered lines and are made of soft, luxury fabrics. Blazers are large and loose, trousers well-cut and womenswear tends to be androgenous, designed for the working woman, although Italian girls love the shorter skirts knotted at the hip. Hang loose in beige!

Armani devotees swear by the comfort and flattering cut of his outfits.

shoulder, softening the contours of the body and eradicating the need for unnecessary darts and fitting lines, offering a less aggressive alternative to those tired of power dressing.

At the beginning of his career his designs were very expensive, using luxurious materials such as alpaca, cashmere and suede. To expand his customer base and meet the increasing demands of a fashion-conscious public for clothes with designer labels, he produced a cheaper range entitled Mani, made out of synthetics so advanced they could not be copied, together with the popular sportswear inspired line, Emporio Armani.

The epitome of post-modern style, Armani clothes may seem anonymous, but their influence has filtered down to the mass-market, redefining all tailoring today, even at the cheapest levels. He is a reclusive personality, rarely granting interviews, and his Milan headquarters at

### GOSSIP

Woe betide the journalist who yawns at an Armani show for, as rumour has it, the maestro himself spies on the audience through a periscope, and instructs his batallions of press officers to shine a torch in the face of any offenders. Could you ever survive the ignominy?

21 via Borgonuovo is more like a fortress than a design studio, with an underground bunker serving as a venue for his catwalk presentations. And yet, even if Italian style at the end of the 20th century is personified by Prada and Gucci's vicehold on the market, for the past twenty years, and probably the next twenty too, the possession of an Armani suit is the tangible trapping of wealth that everyone with a fixation on fashion hankers after.

**1981** Pope John Paul II is shot by a Turkish gunman during his weekly audience in St Peter's Square.

**1986** Norman Foster's Hong Kong and Shanghai Bank building opens; parts of it are made from transparent material following advice from a Feng Shui expert.

**1989** In a ceremony to mark Nigeria's determination to stamp out ivory trading, 12 million tons of elephant tusks, worth $3 million, are burnt in Nairobi.

## 1980s~1990s
# Eurotrash and Tragedy
### Versace

*Gianni VERSACE (1946–97) will be best remembered as the tragic showman whose exuberant designs personified the 'if you've got it, flaunt it' school of fashion of the late 1980s and early 1990s. Every inch a star, he moved in glittering circles and was best mates with all the famous clients he dressed.*

Donatella and Gianni Versace: their mum must have been proud.

He began his fashion career in his mother's atelier when he was eighteen years old, later working for Italian labels Genny and Callaghan before conceiving, designing and launching the Complice label in 1974. In March 1978, Versace the label was born and with it a style of dress that transformed menswear, womenswear, fragrance and ultimately kidswear into fashion's equivalent of rock and roll classics. Versace's signature style combined an understanding of cutting and draping that avoided the stolid beiges and ecrus of his compatriot and rival Armani, opting instead for bright bright satin, chainmail and Rococo prints. He popularized items that had once been considered risqué such as the catsuit, the mini skirt and bustier, and his understanding of draping and bias cutting transformed many a Supermodel into a day-glo version of a Roman goddess.

Liz Hurley: known for her Versace dress and famous boyfriend.

**1992** Serbian forces are accused of 'ethnic cleansing' in Bosnia; they are allegedly ordered to rape and impregnate Muslim women.

**1994** In football, AC Milan win the European Champions' Cup.

**1997** Elton John sings 'Candle in the Wind' at the funeral of Diana, Princess of Wales, shortly after she had comforted him at Versace's funeral.

A galaxy of stars lines up to pay their respects at Versace's funeral in 1997.

## Fashion goes Pop

Just as film stars did in the 1930s and 1940s, pop stars of the 1980s and 1990s have started their own fashion crazes, from Boy George's makeup and ratted hair *(see page 126)* to the Spice Girls' platform trainers *(see page 41)* and Geri Halliwell's Union Jack dress. Madonna *(see also page 95)* started the trend for wearing underwear outside your clothes, roll-down tube skirts that expose the navel, lace tank tops, long black gloves and strings of crucifixes and beads. Michael Jackson got us into wearing a single glove (if you could moonwalk, all the better). Punk *(see pages 108–9)*, Grunge *(see page 135)* and Disco *(see pages 92–3)* fashions were all popularized by pop stars. But there haven't been many people rushing to copy Elton John's lurex suits and ostentatious rhinestone-studded specs. Wonder why? Read pages 110-11 very carefully.

Versace shows were legendary, featuring glass catwalks that protected banks of video screens lip-synching the latest Elton John single, mirrored disco balls that descended from the ceiling and an audience of celebrities to rival the Oscars. His client list read like a *Who's Who* of rock stars and the media, and among his most ardent supporters he counted Elton John, Madonna and the late Diana, Princess of Wales. In 1982, Versace opened a new chapter in his career, making costumes for the theatre, opera and ballet in collaboration with choreographer Maurice Béjart, a passion that was reflected in the theatricality of his designs.

Sadly, the pomp and circumstance that accompanied his career was to come to a brutal end, when the designer was shot dead outside his home on South Ocean Drive in Miami in July 1997. His sister and muse Donatella, who had worked with him since the beginning of his career, has taken over as chief designer for the company to considerable critical acclaim from both fashion editors and clients. Strong colours and clean, fluid lines continue to dominate alongside the historical reinventions and, most of all, the witty sexuality that has always been a Versace signature.

**1981** Ian Paisley is suspended from the House of Commons after referring to the Northern Ireland Secretary in 'unparliamentary language'.

**1982** Alice Walker writes *The Color Purple*; Whoopi Goldberg and Oprah Winfrey will star in the 1985 film.

## 1980s~present
# Italian Rivals
## Prada vs Gucci

*Every era has its fashion icons. In the 1970s Yves Saint Laurent (see pages 90–1) popularized a sanitized ethnic aesthetic that made even the Home Counties housewife consider donning a kaftan. During the 1980s it was the house of Chanel (see pages 42–3) that held sway, as a new breed of yuppies salivated at the thought of all that ostentatious gilt and pearl jewellery. With the 'caring sharing' 1990s, Italian designers stepped into the breach and, if Armani (see pages 124-5) still dressed the career woman, it was Prada and Gucci that dangled the carrot of fashion under her nose.*

Dolce & Gabbana repackage pre-feminist ideals of women for the modern age – and get away with it!

Handbags at dawn.

### Dynamic Duo
Domenico Dolce (b. 1958) and Stefano Gabbana (b. 1962) are the Batman and Robin of Italian fashion, purveying a sexy Sicilian mentality of whores and madonnas to a loyal clientele of voluptuous women. With an eponymous mainline and highly popular D&G diffusion range, the couple specialize in bright, irreverent clothing that often takes inspiration from Southern Italian culture and tradition, and has found favour with celebrities, including Madonna, who loved their rhinestone-spangled bodice.

Like the clashing rocks of fable, Gucci and Prada are the Scylla and Charybdis of contemporary style, sharing a mutual antipathy and a radically different aesthetic. While the Gucci girl is more than likely knocking back tequilas in a night-club, her Prada-clad antithesis is probably discussing philosophy. While Prada purports to have an intellectual approach to fashion, Gucci is hell-bent on having fun. Nevertheless, both labels represent opposite poles of the same luxury market.

Gucci was established in 1906 as a saddlery company and Prada started life in 1913 as a purveyor of fine quality leather goods and imported items. Today both generate the majority of their income from footwear and handbag sales and, in Gucci's case,

**1991** Novelist Barbara Cartland is made a Dame of the British Empire.

**1992** Sears catalogues are delivered to 14 million American homes and sales total $3.3 billion.

**1997** John F. Kennedy, Jr., who had been proclaimed America's Most Eligible Bachelor, marries Carolyn Bessette, who used to work for Calvin Klein Ltd.

novelty items such as dog baskets, handcuffs and cat and dog collars. Both have had chequered histories. Gucci's rise to international fame during the 1950s and 1960s resulted in a company that had licensed its integrity into oblivion by the mid 1980s. Over twenty thousand products bore its name, and too many were bargain-bucket merchandise. In 1988 the fortunes of Gucci took an upturn, when the founder's grandchildren sold their interest to an investment company, which drastically cut the number of licences and brought in a succession of new design directors, including in 1994 the incumbent designer Tom Ford, who has inspired the house to eclipse its former successes.

For Prada, the journey has been less fraught, but when *Miuccia PRADA* (b. 1949) and her husband and business partner Patrizio Bertelli took over the family business in 1978, it was virtually insolvent. Miuccia Prada rediscovered the metal triangle used by her ancestors to monogram

*Kate Moss in Gucci velvet hipsters and silk shirt, 1995.*

luggage (much like the Gucci snaffle that graces shoes and handbags). Using nylon (appropriated from the Italian army's rucksacks and not at that time a fashion staple), she introduced a new dimension in handbags that revolutionized the industry, and an approach to fabrication that has become a hallmark since the first women's ready-to-wear collection in 1989.

In Milan you can gauge the popularity of both brands by the streams of tourists that traipse between the Gucci flagship store on Via Montenapoleone and the Prada boutique on Via Andrea Maffei. Needless to say, they're both doing nicely, thank you.

**1983** Valentino designs a black and white check coat to be worn with black court shoes with black and white checked soles.

**1988** Jean-Michel Basquiat dies of a drug overdose; he began his career as a graffiti artist on the New York subway before his famous collaborations with Andy Warhol.

**1991** In Southampton, two artists admit that they were responsible for the creation of some corn circles but thousands of devotees worldwide still think there's an extraterrestrial explanation.

1980s~present

# Conservative Chic

## German fashion

*While London is wrestling with the latest shock tactics employed by a young designer scarcely out of college, Paris is welcoming the newest influx of Japanese talent and Milan is wondering which celebrities will turn up at the Versace show, German fashion is dressing the world in tasteful conservatism. For the fashion wannabe, the wealthy city of Düsseldorf (nicknamed Dallasdorf by its detractors) may not symbolize one of European fashion's heartlands but, chances are, your local boutique contains as many Teutonic labels as it does discreetly chic French brands or racy Italian numbers.*

Jil Sander coat demonstrating the plain classicism for which she's known.

### Olsen

Co-ordinate and knitwear house Olsen is a classic German success story. Founded in 1901, it was a no-brand label until 1995, when the family-owned business decided to launch itself as a label, and now generates an income of 180 million DM per annum, with thousands of stockists across Europe and North America. Not bad for a few jumpers, when British designers gain acres of publicity but few sales – and that's Germany's secret.

For Düsseldorf is home to CPD, the world's largest fashion trade fair, that encompasses fourteen halls, each one packed with merchandise ranging in scope from elegant eveningwear to ultra-traditional dirndls that could have walked off the set of a *Heidi* re-make. And for the buyer, it is one of the main focal points of the commercial season, especially for those whose customer places fashion on an equal footing with the purchase of a new fridge freezer.

You see, German fashion doesn't necessarily revolve around *Karl LAGERFELD (see pages 78–9)* and *Jil SANDER (b. 1943)*, both of whom choose to show outside their native country, but the blockbusters of ready-to-wear such as Escada, Mondi and Betty Barclay, that have enormous appeal for a woman of a certain age, who no longer wishes to wear the extreme fashions on the catwalks but isn't ready to become a frump either. Despite a reputation for being more akin to trimming hedge rather than cutting edge, German fashion is sociologically far more important than its critics would have us believe, because it deals in strict realities rather than

**1995** 'Rogue trader' Nick Leeson brings down Barings Bank after running up losses of £620 million dealing in the Singapore futures market.

**1996** In Norway, Hege Solli makes a wedding train that is 670 feet long.

**1998** In the UK, Delia Smith gets rich from teaching people how to boil an egg.

unobtainable fantasies. That broad-shouldered blazer with insignia and gold buttons, bought in the boom of the 1980s, is probably from Mondi; the nippy suit that the mother-of-the-bride is wearing was probably designed in the Munich studios of Escada; and the comfortable blouse and matching skirt that's perfect for a Sunday pub lunch and a drive in the country is probably Betty Barclay.

Ask a German clothing manufacturer about the industry, and they'll wax lyrical about the elasticated panels on 'easy-fit' trousers, the popularity of casualwear or the wash-and-go benefits of new fibres such as Tencel. Ask the retailer and they'll tell you about prompt deliveries, great fit and a quality that has made brands with unfortunate-sounding names such as Mothwurf as desirable as Prada at the boutique in Lower Ribblethwaite. No-one will deny that this is grass roots fashion, but every garden has a lawn, and there is often limited space for half hardy 'designer' annuals. Instead German fashion is comfortable, classic

Kate Moss in Jil Sander's 'just out of bed and can't think what to wear' look.

> ## FASHION ESSENTIALS
>
> Jil Sander was a German pioneer of minimalism in the mid 1980s, using simple, clean-cut shapes, often adapted from menswear. She uses top-quality fabrics in neutral colours, producing classic trouser suits and must-have jackets that never seem to date. Basler, Ara and Bianca are less innovative German firms that successfully target the middle classes.

Middle-class comforts: Nehru jacket and trousers by Betty Barclay.

and not always as frumpy as it is painted by the media.

Escada has employed consultants such as American *Todd OLDHAM* (b. 1961) to pep up its colourful image; Mondi has taken on Maggie Norris from Ralph Lauren *(see page 104)* to revamp the house style; and formerly conservative brands such as Strenesse have upped the fashion content of their collections by showing in Milan.

German fashion (with few exceptions) is unlikely to set the creative juices flowing but scrape away the glitz and you're more likely to find a neat two-piece trouser suit than a Galliano extravaganza.

**1991** The style of dance called 'vogueing', developed in Harlem by black and Latino drag queens who parody the strut of high-fashion mannequins, is captured in the film *Paris is Burning*.

**1992** Boxer Mike Tyson is sentenced to six years in jail for raping beauty queen Desiree Washington.

**1993** Kim Basinger has to pay $8.9 million after refusing to appear in *Boxing Helena* as a woman who is kept in a box after her limbs have been cut off.

1990~1998

# Supermodels
## Out-glitzing Hollywood

*When Linda Evangelista declared 'We don't get out of bed for less than $10,000 a day', it became apparent to the world and his dog that a new breed of model had arrived – the supermodel. Based on the equation 'image equals income', the modelling élite of the early 1990s found they could write their own ticket –and frequently did.*

A British *Vogue* cover of 1990 with Naomi, Linda, Tatjana, Christy and Cindy.

The term 'supermodel' first cropped up in the late 1980s when, despite a recession, the glamour and superstar status of certain models was seen as enough to carry all-important brand identities and keep luxury labels in profit. Most designers were happy to invest the astronomical figures asked for because they saw the returns. Slinky and Amazonian Tatjana Patitz, classically beautiful Christy Turlington, All-American girl Cindy Crawford, androgynous and chameleon-like Linda Evangelista, feline Naomi Campbell (who became the first-ever black

### The Dosh

Money, money, money. Christy Turlington's contract with Calvin Klein cost him $3 million while, at her peak, Claudia Schiffer was grossing $12 million a year. Cindy Crawford makes a fortune as America's favourite calendar girl and Versace had to cough up £30,000 for each supermodel's appearance on the Milan catwalks. Less successful ventures have included Naomi Campbell's brief and disastrous foray into novel-writing and, even worse, into pop music; and the supermodels' fast-food brainwave The Fashion Café never really took off (food and supermodels not being the most obvious association).

Rumours of cattiness on the catwalk have been categorically denied.

**1995** Julia Roberts, Tim Robbins, Cher and a host of stars feature in Robert Altman's *Prêt a Porter*, set in Paris Fashion Week.

**1996** Jessica Dubroff, aged seven, is killed trying to become the youngest person to fly a plane across the US.

**1997** The first lesbian beauty contest in the world is held in London.

cover girl for French *Vogue*) and Germanic blonde Claudia Schiffer, all seemed to possess the X factor that made the public rush out and buy. Photographer *Steven Meisel* (b. 1954) dubbed Turlington, Campbell and Evangelista with the iconic term 'the Trinity' and was influential in developing and maintaining their fascination for the public.

Kate Moss having her breakfast. Or it could be lunch. Or dinner.

## Twiggy Mark II

Kate Moss re-wrote the definition of the model. In complete contrast to the supermodels of the early 1990s, she is skinny, five foot six and has slightly bowed legs. But by the age of twenty-one she had a $2-million contract with Calvin Klein (*see page 104*). Discovered by influential fashion photographer Corrine Day (*see page 34*), her easy-come easy-go attitude has made her perfect for recent campaigns for Calvin Klein, notably for his fragrance CKOne. While Moss has many of the trappings of the old supermodel (dates movie stars, likes to party), she is very different from her pneumatic predecessors. She has a sort of super-ordinariness that marks her out as the obvious backlash against the rest of the breed. She's also (bitch, bitch) a bit younger than the rest.

## GOSSIP

The supermodels love lives soon eclipsed the clothes, with Naomi Campbell serially dating anyone who headlined from Mike Tyson and Robert De Niro to Spanish flamenco dancer Joaquim Cortéz (they didn't speak a word of each other's language); there was the on-off-on-again relationship of Kate Moss and Johnny Depp and reports of them bathing in champagne; Linda's romance with Kyle MacLachlan; Helena Christienson and Michael Hutchence; and the bizarre marriage of Cindy Crawford and Richard Gere, which ended shortly after a advertisement declaring their undying love had been published in the *Times* newspaper.

The cult of the supermodel grew and grew. George Michael enshrined them in his music video 'Freedom', forever endearing them to the MTV generation. Bodyguards were employed, magazines dedicated, books written for and about them and supermodel dolls created.

However, reports of tantrums over who got to wear which frock, public outrage at the huge fees, and a new breed of ordinary model heralded by Kate Moss all hastened the decline of the supermodel towards the end of the decade. So far no charitable foundation has been set up to try and save this rare breed from extinction.

**1991** The film *Groundhog Day* features a single day repeated over and over and over again in a small town in Pennsylvania.

**1992** Woody Allen and Mia Farrow split up after she finds out he is having an affair with her 21-year-old adopted daughter Soon-Yi.

**1993** Rock star Prince changes his name, becoming The Artist Formerly Known as Prince.

1991~1999
# Turning Fashion Inside Out
## Deconstruction

Margiela uses dummies in place of models. Uh huh!

*For a subject that is notoriously non-academic, the term 'deconstruction' lends a faintly intellectual air to what is essentially a different way of looking at fashion. In essence it is the science of looking at a garment in its component parts and constructing new shapes from a traditional form: a jacket may be turned inside out, exposing the seams and lining; raw edges and unfinished hems become focal points rather than examples of poor dressmaking; and, in its most extreme form, a simple piece of fabric wrapped around the torso becomes a skirt.*

How to a make an old sheet look chic: dress by Ann Demeulemeester.

Now you understand the basics, it's time for the origins or, more specifically, the city of origin: Antwerp in Belgium, a fashion beacon in a country better known for mussels, chips and chocolate. This provincial city has produced some of the most forward-thinking designers of the late 1990s, most notably *Martin MARGIELA* (b. 1957), *Ann DEMEULEMEESTER* (b. 1959). *Dries van NOTEN* (b. 1958), and Walter van Bierendonck of W&LT fame. All have been proponents of deconstruction and have

### FASHION ESSENTIALS

☞ For the Margiela look, rip the sleeves off your jackets, mix antique and floral fabrics, and turn the whole ensemble inside-out so the seams show.

☞ For the Demeulemeester ensemble, pair hippie fabrics with stark long coats, or halter vests with low-slung skirts or trousers.

☞ Van Noten favours layered jersey and silk knits, duster coats and jackets buttoned on the diagonal.

**1995** Footballer Eric Cantona attacks a fan with a kung-fu kick.

**1997** A skydiver survives a 12,000-feet fall after his parachute failed to open, when he lands on top of his instructor, who dies.

**1999** Monica Lewinsky's book about her relationship with President Clinton hits the bestseller lists, although everyone has heard the stories countless times already.

redefined conventional tailoring and finishing techniques, previously the province of ateliers in Paris and Milan or London's Savile Row *(see pages 20–1)*. All were graduates of the Antwerp Academy, Belgium's equivalent of Central Saint Martin's in London *(see page 136)* or Parson's in New York, colleges that have a reputation for breeding design superstars.

## BUILDING BLOCKS

And yet, despite a similar point of origin, each has a different handwriting that encompasses a sombre, north European aesthetic but retains an individuality of its own. For Dries Van Noten the keywords are ethnicity and colour, combining a wild cacophany of print and texture on a long layered silhouette. Demeulemeester is famous for her unusual juxtapositions of fabrics and innovative shapes. Martin Margiela (probably the high priest of decon-struction) has radically challenged our notions of design by relocating armholes on the body, turning silhouettes upside down, and exposing the inner tailoring methods on jackets and coats. And, as a reward for spear-heading an avant-garde approach to fashion design, he has been appointed designer for the luxury goods house Hermès. It seems that what was once deemed an underground concept, appealing solely to the most ardent fashion victims, has now been adopted by the haute bourgeoisie.

### Shabby chic

More than just an excuse for looking scruffy, Grunge evolved in the early 1990s as an anti-fashion statement by streetwise teenagers and pop stars, characterized by torn clothing, garments that were miles too big or way too small, mismatched colours and patterns. Always quick to jump on the bandwagon, Madonna adopted Grunge looks with lank hair, floaty frocks and ripped jackets. Devotees originally selected their outfits in charity shops until some designers picked up on the trend and killed it stone dead by bringing it to the high street.

Nirvana, Seattle's proponents of Grunge, forgot to brush their hair before coming out. *Nevermind*!

Wacko Jacko's face may be perfect but his jeans need mending.

**1997** It pours with rain as Britain finally hands over the colony of Hong Kong to China amid great ceremony.

**1997** MI5 advertise for trainee spies in the British press.

**1998** The Tamworth Two dominate the British media after these intrepid pigs escape from the slaughter house.

1997~1999

# Cool Britannia
## Originality and street style

Making a song and dance about British fashion: a McQueen show.

*Once an event catering for toothy debs and tired ballgowns, London Fashion Week has transformed the UK fashion industry from a pit stop into an essential sojourn for the international buying and media communities. To list the talents the city has spawned would be absurd; the secret that lies behind the success of London as a fashion capital is its diversity, from the international big guns such as Alexander MCQUEEN (b. 1969) and John GALLIANO (b. 1960) at Givenchy and Dior respectively, to the countless British design graduates that fuel the imagination of many household names overseas.*

P in-pointing what has generated such a hotbed of creativity is an onerous task. Maybe it's something in the water, or perhaps the economic optimism generated by the birth of New Labour and Tony Blair, but the capital has long been associated with strong street fashion links. Visit any trendy nightclub and you're likely to bump into the likes of Jean-Paul Gaultier *(see page 95)* frantically sketching in the corner, or a Japanese camera crew criss-crossing the dancefloor. But it is the British fashion colleges that really deserve the credit for launching wave upon wave of new designer names onto the international circuit, and particularly Central Saint Martin's (see box).

Despite an increasingly lukewarm reaction from the domestic press, who are tired

Who said the clothes had to be wearable?

**1998** Hanif Kureishi writes a novel about a man leaving his partner and two children, shortly after he himself has left his partner and two children.

**1999** David Beckham and 'Posh Spice' have a son, whom they call Brooklyn.

**1999** Period drama triumphs in the film awards, with *Shakespeare in Love* sweeping the Oscars and *Elizabeth* hoovering up the BAFTAs.

Showman extraordinaire: Galliano's club-style catwalk.

## STYLE ICON
★

*Deep in the heart of Soho lies Central Saint Martin's College of Art and Design, the alma mater of British creativity. Once accused of 'agro chic' because of its hard-edged tailoring output, it has also been responsible for the bright ethnicity of designer Matthew Williamson or the arch historicism of Antonio Berardi. Its mantra teaches the dual disciplines of business acumen (because so many designers went bust in the 1980s) and creativity; past students include Galliano, McQueen, McCartney and others too numerous to mention.*

of hyping their own country, and the efforts of the French and Americans who lurk in the shadows of London Fashion Week with offers of big-bucks catwalk shows overseas. London continues to thrive as a fashion capital. Streetwear brands such as Vexed Generation, YMC and Maharishi have re-educated the sportswear consumer into a modern, minimalist mode of dress, while wannabe bohemians are spoilt for choice with a plethora of boutiques such as The Cross, Fashion Gallery and Voyage (the latter claims the Pope is the only celebrity not to have left the store clutching a confection of velvet and lace).

Finally there is London Fashion Week itself, acting as an incubator for talent. As yet British fashion may not have the selling power of Armani or Calvin Klein but as the public become increasingly hungry for new design, soon we'll be leading the world in sales as well as bright ideas.

Stella McCartney's glittering career: all the way from St Martin's to Chloé.

**2006** The bustle makes a comeback – the bigger the better. Fashionable shops and clubs have to widen their doorways so women can squeeze through.

**2018** Genetically modified flowers hit the market; they bloom and give off scent all year round.

**2024** Women no longer have to try on clothes in changing rooms as most stores have installed hologram machines that show them what they'll look like.

21st century

# The Shape of Things to Come
## Futuristic fashion

*It is the beginning of the third millennium, and yet in some ways our thoughts on the future of fashion are governed by the concepts of futurism made popular by the 'Space Age' contingent of designers from the 1960s (see pages 88–9). In fact, tomorrow's designers are equally likely to be influenced by street culture as an image of Jane Fonda's Barbarella clad in a perspex bodysuit.*

Fashion today has become disseminated to such an extent that neither the catwalks nor the high street can claim to provide a significant lead to the populace. Trends remain in circulation for much longer and garments that started life in a couture salon may end up on a market stall, albeit executed in polyester rather than hand-embroidered satin. The term 'fashion' has broadened its tentacles to encompass the food we eat, the interiors we live in and the plants we grow in our gardens. 'Lifestyle' marketing has decreed that to be aesthetically fulfilled one must inhabit an environment lifted from the pages of *Martha Stewart Living*.

Our obsession with buying into an unobtainable dream has led to a creative malaise. Retail analysts describe today's mass-market as 'risk averse': each chain store design studio will wait to ensure that its new collection has lifted the appropriate looks from the international catwalks, resulting in ranges that have little creative integrity and a limited appeal to the consumers (who schlep around rails of identikit merchandise differentiated only by the label at the back of the neck).

Space cadet: Jane Fonda in the sci-fi soft-porn film *Barbarella* (1967).

**2039** Oasis play a comeback tour; Noel and Liam are now in their sixties.

**2051** At his seventieth birthday celebrations, Britain's King William announces that he is leaving his wife for a seventeen-year-old lap dancer.

**2065** Anti-ageing creams have become so successful that it is impossible to tell someone's age without checking their electronic ID.

## FASHION ESSENTIALS

Buy basics from The Gap, shoes from Prada and accessories from a fleamarket – or basics from Prada, accessories from The Gap and shoes from a fleamarket – it no longer matters.

It may look like a costume for a Russian shot-putter but it's actually a Prada creation.

If a Maoist aesthetic has begun to homogenize fashion in the mass market, the flipside is a return to craftsmanship and the re-birth of the cottage industry, that the big guns of international fashion cannot compete against. Small boutiques, specializing in one-off designs created on a sewing machine in a spare bedroom, are a growth area within the market, and younger designers are pulling away from logo-based fashion. As the customer becomes increasingly demanding, levels of quality within the market as a whole are rising. Phrases such as 'low impact luxury' have been coined to describe the simple cashmere vest, which may not look exciting but inspires confidence in the wearer through the innate quality of manufacture and materials. The pashmina, a fine cashmere security blanket so beloved by the fashion press during long-haul flights, has now been introduced by high-street giant Marks & Spencer, and is currently the best-selling article in their London flagship store. Nasty nylon and drip-dry shirts have been replaced by synthetics so advanced they seem natural, or by the homespun itself. Lambswool alone is no longer good enough – it has to be at least a cashmere blend.

Each decade produces the cry 'Fashion is Dead' but the truth is that its persona has radically altered. Today fashion dominates our media; it is a dream that everyone can afford, and it doesn't matter if your look is 'charity shop chic'. Regardless of where we shop or what we buy, beauty remains in the eye of the beholder – even if you're wearing coloured contact lenses.

Kirsten Johnson and the indispensable pashmina.

**1987** The world population reaches 5 billion, double the number in 1950.

**1990** The Human Genome Project begins, a worldwide collaboration of scientists attempting to map out the complete genetic makeup of human beings.

**1994** Three friends hail a taxi from London, UK, to Cape Town, South Africa. The journey takes more than four months and costs them £40,210.

1980s~2000

# Fashion Atlas
## A tale of four cities

Just a few cosmetic details.

*Imagine just for a moment that you have £10,000 to spend on clothes. And what's more, thanks to the fashion fairy, you have a round-the-world ticket to visit the leading fashion capitals, where the ardent shopper can sample the most elegant and tawdry that the fashion world has to offer.*

### NEW YORK

First stop New York, where Midtown emporia such as Barneys, Bergdorfs and Saks are the envy of the world. Invest in cosmetics and beauty care, cheaper than in Europe, and brands such as Calvin Klein and Ralph Lauren. For the true label junkie on a budget, Canal Street is a forger's paradise. Purchase a fake Rolex for $15 and check out the Prada rucksacks that look good until the logo falls off. Finally explore SoHo and Greenwich Village, both crammed with small boutiques offering the best in vintage clothing and up-and-coming designers.

### MILAN

Take a tram into the city centre, and you'll probably strap-hang with a model on her way to an appointment. Head for the city's two main shopping streets: Via Della Spiga, home to Prada and Dolce & Gabbana, and Via Montenapoleone, where Gucci and Versace attract busloads of Japanese tourists. And, if neither takes your fancy, the surrounding square mile is home to shops offering the best from fashion's big guns. Two things worth remembering: domestically produced luxury goods are often cheaper in Italy than abroad, and despite the intimidating nature of the city, the shop assistants are the friendliest in Europe (even if you're in a pair of jeans and an old sweatshirt).

From window-shopping to arcade-hopping; big names mean austere elegance.

**1995** According to the British Meteorological Office, this is the warmest year on record, raising fears about the effects of global warming.

**1998** Eastern European models are all the rage, with young stars picked from the streets of Moscow, Krakow and Prague.

**1999** Breitling Orbiter is the first manned balloon to fly right round the globe.

Paris flea market to London bag lady: the bank manager's nightmare.

## PARIS

While Milanese shops excel in smoked-glass windows and immaculate cream carpets, the inhabitant of the typical Parisian boutique is a vendeuse who will glance at the bystander over pince-nez, before producing the perfect lace camisole from one of innumerable wooden drawers under the counter. And, if the bijou is not to your liking, a new breed of retailers such as Collette caters for the fashion cognoscenti (read victims) by offering the cream of international cutting-edge design, sold in tandem with more affordable nick-nacks and a rather pretentious water bar, for the diet conscious.

Finally no visit to Paris is complete without taking a trip to Tati, the cut-price department store whose gingham carrier bags hold treasures such as leather jeans at £15, and whose bargain bin piles of clothing are a fun antidote to the 'can I help you madom' school of assistants that populate the city. Just plunge in and take your pick, because who cares if it falls apart when it only cost a fiver?

## LONDON

Lastly London, home to Cool Britannia and much more besides. Check out the best in affordably priced chainstores such as Top Shop, Warehouse and Oasis for the best looks off the catwalks at prices within the reach of the average consumer, and for something more special, the city has innumerable small boutiques specializing in one-offs and innovative design that you won't find anywhere else. Bear in mind that London is a series of villages, where neighbouring areas can be as radically different as national borders, each one throwing up its own stylistic approach– if you want a suit head for Savile Row; a sari, Southall; likewise, if you can stomach the hordes of tourists following the 'Notting Hill' trail made popular by the movie, the Friday and Saturday market at Portobello is a pricey but amusing way to see London at play, and great for vintage and second-hand clothes. If designer gear is more your thing then Knightsbridge, home to department stores Harrods and Harvey Nichols, should be your first stop.

# Index